JAPAN

OCTOPUS BOOKS

Acknowledgments

Editor: Penny Summers
Art Editor: David Rowley
Designer: Sue Storey
Production Controller: Trevor Jones

Special Photography: James Murphy
Food Preparation: Dolly Meers
Styling: Andrea Lambton, Sarah Wiley
Illustrations: Sally Davies

The publishers wish to thank the following for providing photographs for this book:

Octopus/Martin Brigdale page 11, 19, 21, 23, 27, 31, 37, 38–39, 53, 55;
Octopus/Robert Golden 25, 51, 61.

ACE Photo Agency/Richard Walker page 5;
Robert Harding/Picture Library 7.

All recipes are for 4 servings unless otherwise stated

First published 1987 by
Octopus Books Limited
59 Grosvenor Street
London W1

ISBN 0 7064 3098 0

Printed in Hong Kong

Contents

JAPAN

For centuries, Japan was a closed port and it was not subject to foreign influence until quite recently. This probably explains how it developed such a unique, elegant style of cooking. Despite the proximity to China and the use of many similar ingredients, the Japanese approach to cooking, and the resulting flavours, are entirely different from the Chinese.

There is probably no other cuisine in the world which practises 'culinary art' to the same extent as the Japanese. A strong awareness of natural colour, symmetry and general appearance of each prepared food is crucial – visual feasting is part of the traditional meal. Japanese dishes are made pleasing by the artistic way in which the food is arranged and garnished on beautiful ceramic plates or bowls. Hand-crafted serving dishes and bowls, often specially created by a potter, are carefully selected for each item of food. The Japanese have a talent for arranging the food and garnish to display contrast of colour, shape and texture; seasonal fresh flowers and leaves are often used to decorate a dish.

4

Opposite: *a breathtaking view of Mount Fuji on a clear day.*

Each ingredient for a Japanese meal is prepared separately and thus, even when served together, the individual flavours and colours are retained. The Japanese have a great reverence for food, and Japan is probably one of the few countries in the world where people will pay any price to savour the very 'first' sweet strawberry, fragrant *matsutake* (pine mushroom) or juicy melon of the season. These are often packed individually in special boxes, with elaborate cushioning, and sold as gifts. A great deal of time and effort goes into producing these gourmet delights.

Although Japanese food is renowned for the care and effort taken over its presentation, it is also gastronomically distinguished. A major characteristic of this cuisine is its reliance on natural flavours: only the best and freshest of ingredients are used; cooking is kept to a minimum; seasonings are delicate and fragrant. The Japanese take extreme pride in growing the best fruit and vegetables; in fishing for only the freshest seafood; in hand-massaging their cattle and feeding them beer to produce the world's most expensive, beautifully marbled and tender beef. The average housewife makes a daily trip to the market to buy the freshest foods for her table, even if she has a refrigerator.

The Japanese are close to nature, and the four seasons are always present in the imagination of the cook. There is also a strong vegetarian tradition in modern-day Japan, despite a decline in Buddhism, and in most Japanese meals you will find three times as many vegetable dishes as meat.

For the Westerner, it is quite simple to prepare a meal as it would be served in a Japanese home. When it comes to home cooking, most Japanese mealtimes are rather casual: all the dishes are placed on the table at the same time and everyone helps themselves.

Formal cooking is very distinct from home cooking. Formal dishes, called *kaiseki ryori* (see below), are mainly served at special restaurants and tea ceremony parties. However, there are still similarities: in the freshness of ingredients, meticulous preparation, the minimal use of seasoning during cooking and in careful presentation.

In most modern homes, meals are eaten round a conventional dining table; but in a traditional Japanese home, diners are barefoot and either kneel or sit cross-legged around a dining table that is as low as a Western coffee table. In the entrance of every home, shoes are removed and slippers put on, so dining at floor level is a very clean custom. The diners sit on cushions placed on the *tatami* (straw mat) floor.

Each person has a bowl of boiled rice on his left-hand side and a bowl of soup on his right. *Hashi* (chopsticks) are placed immediately in front of each place setting. One or two dishes are served in individual bowls, immediately behind the rice and soup, while the remainder are served on larger dishes in the centre of the table. A typical Japanese lunch or dinner would consist of soup followed by several fish, chicken or meat and vegetable dishes – one steamed or barbecued, one fried and so on – served with rice and pickled vegetables or a salad. The vegetables or salad would be served in small portions, as a taste supplement.

Because the look of the food on the table is so important, dishes, bowls and plates are chosen to harmonize with the shape and colour of what they contain, and with the season of the year, rather than to match each other.

After a traditional dinner there is a mountain of little dishes and plates to be cleared. Knives and forks are not used for eating; the food is cut into small pieces during preparation and eaten with chopsticks, with the exception of whole fish which can be separated easily with chopsticks when cooked.

Japanese cooking is relatively simple. Most dishes are cooked in advance and served at room temperature, since there are sometimes only two burners on the gas stove. In the past, few Japanese kitchens had ovens, but in recent years, portable ones have become available. In fact, Japan was the first country to introduce microwave ovens for domestic use.

It is interesting to compare the different cuisines of Japan and China: while the Chinese mix ingredients together, the Japanese keep them separate so that each can be savoured for itself. Most Japanese food is grilled, steamed, simmered or occasionally deep-fried, whereas the Chinese prefer stir-frying in oil.

Kaiseki Ryori

This formal style of cooking developed from the special dishes which were created for the original Japanese tea ceremony, about three hundred years ago. Food is presented in a particular order determined by the cooking method, and the four seasons dictate the selection of ingredients to be served. In a formal *kaiseki* meal, the courses follow one another in a set order: clear soup, appetizer, simmered dish, broiled dish, meat dish, vegetables, large fried dish, boiled rice and finally *sunomono* (vinegared vegetables), *miso* soup and green tea.

Nowadays, *kaiseki* dishes are only served in first-class Japanese restaurants called *ryotei*, although at special parties and on ceremonial occasions, such as New Year's Day, Children's Day and the Equinox, meals at home are traditionally served with a little more formality.

Etiquette

There are few formal rules of etiquette to follow, but certain traditions are kept. It is customary, for example, to offer your guests rolled towels with which to wipe their hands (and face if wished) before eating. In winter these towels are dampened with very hot water, in summer with iced water. Serving utensils are not used, simply because all food is meticulously cut into small, bite-size pieces and arranged in bowls or plates before it is brought to the table. Chopsticks should not be placed across a bowl or stuck into rice (this is a sign of mourning). Grains of rice should always be lifted to the mouth between the chopsticks.

Japanese Festivals

Certain holidays are celebrated in grand style, and New Year is probably the most important of these. Food is prepared and placed in beautiful tiered, lacquered boxes. Friends, relatives and neighbours come to greet each other and food and drink are served. A rice patty made from glutinous (sweet) rice is dropped into *ozoni* (a special New Year's soup). So sacred is this holiday

A patchwork of fields indicates intensive cultivation near Kyoto.

that the 'o' is put before the word *zoni* to give the honorific form of the word. *Osechi ryori* is a carefully planned combination of foods for the New Year feast. During a one-week period of celebration, the shops are closed and virtually all of Japan is at a standstill.

Girls' Day is traditionally celebrated each year on 3rd March – the significance of this date being the association between the Japanese words for 'three' and 'beauty', the sound *mi* meaning both. The maternal grandparents of a baby girl should present her with a set of dolls at birth, called *ohina-sama*, and these are brought out and displayed on Girls' Day. On this day food is chosen for its beauty and colour.

Children's Day in May (formerly Boy's Day) is celebrated with fragrant cherry leaves wrapped around special rice cakes.

The Japanese still observe a number of culinary traditions like these, despite the Western influences of recent years.

Ingredients

The name for rice is *gohan*, which is the generic word for 'meal'. Rice is served at all meals. So valued is this 'staff of life' that the Japanese have an old saying, *tsukiyo no kome no meshi*, which means 'moonlight and boiled rice' – one never tires of eating even a simple meal of boiled rice by moonlight. When you have become acquainted with Japanese cuisine, you will appreciate the full meaning of this ancient proverb. Plain boiled Japanese rice does have an especially satisfying flavour, and is delicious by itself.

Unlike Indian or Chinese rice, Japanese rice is the short-grain variety. It is normally boiled and, when cooked, clings together. It is essential to eat every grain of rice that is served to you, as it would be considered unforgivable to waste this revered food.

Fish, shellfish and seaweed are plentiful, and the varieties available numerous, so it is not surprising that these foods play a dominant role in Japanese cookery. There are almost as many types of seaweed as there are fish, and packets of dried seaweed can be purchased in the West from Japanese supermarkets or oriental stores.

Despite the limited area available for agriculture in Japan, there is an abundance of fruit and vegetables, including many that are distinctly Japanese. As is the rule with most Japanese food, vegetables must be young, tender and absolutely fresh. Most Japanese cooks shop daily and will throw away any vegetables that are even slightly sub-standard.

Japanese salads are usually composed of cooked vegetables that have been pickled or vinegared, unlike Western salads which are made with raw ingredients. Pickling is an important way of preserving produce, and vinegared vegetables complement the flavours of Japanese cooking superbly. Vegetable byproducts, such as those made from soy beans, are particularly important in Japanese cooking: almost no dish is complete without the addition of soy sauce, and *tofu* (soy bean curd) is used extensively.

It is essential to use *shoyu* (Japanese light soy sauce) in these recipes; to use Chinese soy sauce instead would ruin the flavour of the dish. The same applies to *miso* (Japanese soy bean paste), which is entirely different from Chinese soy bean paste.

Sake (rice wine) is the traditional accompaniment to Japanese food. It is served warm and enjoyed throughout the meal. Green tea is a national habit. It is served frequently during the day and at meal times in fragile ceramic tea cups without handles. Green tea has a very clean, delicate flavour, and is therefore well-suited to Japanese cuisine.

Special Ingredients

Abur-age: Fried bean curd, available ready-prepared in packages or frozen. It is often thinly sliced and included in salads and soups, or opened to make a pouch which is then filled with *sushi* (vinegared rice).

Agar-agar: Known as *kanten* in Japan, this is a kind of seaweed which is available in long white strands or powdered form. Use in very small quantities, as a little will quickly set a large volume of liquid. It has almost no taste or colour. Powdered gelatine may be substituted: allow 4 tablespoons gelatine to 25 g (1 oz) agar-agar. Available from oriental stores and some health food shops.

Akamiso: Red soy bean paste.

Azuki: Red beans. Sweetened azuki beans are available in cans.

Bamboo shoots: The tender young shoots which appear at the base of the bamboo are gathered at the end of the rainy season, parboiled and canned. Once opened, and with regular changes of cold water, they will keep for about seven days. Canned bamboo shoots are available sliced or unsliced.

Bean curd: Known as *tofu* in Japan, bean curd or cake is made from puréed soy beans. It is soft and white with a cheese-like texture, which ranges from firm to 'silken'. Bean curd is high in protein and very low in fat, and is therefore highly nutritious. It has a bland flavour but combines well with other ingredients. Fresh bean curd, sold in cakes 6 cm (2½ inches) square and 1 cm (½ inch) thick, will keep fresh for several days if stored in the refrigerator. For *fried bean curd*, see **Abur-age**.

Beni-shoga: Sweet pickled ginger root traditionally used to garnish *sushi* (vinegared rice) dishes.

Burdock: See **Gobo**.

Daikon: Also called Japanese radish, the daikon is a long white radish which has a crisp texture. It is used extensively as a garnish when grated, sliced and carved, and as a cooked vegetable. Icicle radish makes an acceptable substitute.

Dashi: Made with preflaked dried bonito flakes (*katsuo bushi*, q.v.) and seaweed (*konbu*, q.v.), dashi is the basic Japanese stock and is used in many recipes. Dashi is easy to make but sachets of instant dashi mix, which sell under the name of *dashi-no-moto*, are available for the sake of convenience.

Ginger: Fresh root ginger, sometimes referred to as green ginger. Peel before using, then slice, crush or chop finely. To keep fresh: peel, then wash and place in a jar; cover with pale dry sherry, seal and store in the refrigerator. Ground ginger is not an acceptable substitute, but dried root ginger may be used, in which case the quantity should be decreased.

Gingko nuts: These nuts have a delicate flavour and texture and are widely available in cans. Both the shell and inner skin should be removed before use.

Glutinous rice: This is known as *mochigome* in Japan, and is also sometimes referred to as sticky rice. It is a short-grain rice that becomes very sticky when cooked. Used in stuffings, cakes and puddings.

Glutinous rice flour: This is called *mochiko* in Japan. It

1) Abur-age (deep-fried bean curd); 2) assorted garnishes, including grated daikon (Japanese radish), lemon shreds, carrot and tomato flowers, green pepper strips and pickled ginger shreds; 3) assorted seaweed, placed on a sheet of nori (dried laver paper), with kanpyo (dried shaved gourd strings) in the corner; 4) soba noodles; 5) dried plums; 6) pine nuts; 7) gingko nuts; 8) azuki beans; 9) sesame seeds; 10) moulded wasabi paste (Japanese horseradish); 11) selection of sushi; 12) dried persimmons; 13) seaweed tied with kanpyo; 14) Japanese short-grain rice; 15) rice cakes; 16) shiso leaves; 17) shiitake mushrooms; 18) chilli oil; 19) quail's eggs; 20) selection of sashimi; 21) enokitake mushrooms; 22) lotus root; 23) selection of fresh seafood; 24) selection of fruit and vegetables, including star fruit, gobo (burdock) and lotus roots.

8

is made from ground glutinous rice.

Gobo: Commonly known as burdock, this is a long, slender root vegetable with a crunchy texture. Both fresh and canned burdock is available. If wished, you can use *jicama* instead.

Goma: See **Sesame.**

Goma jio: To prepare these salted sesame seeds, dry fry 1 tablespoon black sesame seeds in a hot frying pan until they 'jump', shaking the pan constantly. Transfer to a bowl, then sprinkle with 2 teaspoons salt.

Gyoza skins: These are round in shape. Wonton skins may be used as a substitute.

Hakusai: See **Napa cabbage.**

Harusame: Soy bean noodles. These can be used instead of mung bean threads (q.v.).

Hijiki: Brown algae seaweed.

Kanpyo: Long, dried, ribbon-like strips from an edible gourd. They are used for tying and securing foods, or can be cooked with vegetables or fish. They should be salted and soaked before use.

Kanten: See **Agar-agar.**

Kasu: Rice wine lees, sold in 2.25 kg (5 lb) blocks in oriental stores.

Katsuo-bushi: The dried fillet of a bonito fish. When flaked, it is one of the most essential ingredients in Japanese cooking, as it is used as the basic flavouring in *dashi* (q.v.). It is also used as a garnish and is available preflaked.

Konbu: Dried kelp (seaweed). This is a basic ingredient used to flavour *dashi* (q.v.) and other dishes. It is also used as a vegetable in its own right.

Kon-nyaku: A dense, gelatinous cake prepared from arum roots. Available in packages or cans.

Lotus root: Known as *renkon* in Japan, this is available fresh, dried or canned.

Matcha: The powdered green tea used for the traditional Japanese tea ceremony. It is made from the most tender leaves of the first spring picking, and is processed by a very expensive and laborious method.

Mirin: A sweet rice wine with a very low alcohol content. It is used in many Japanese dishes to add a subtle sweetness. If unavailable, use 1 teaspoon sugar for each tablespoon mirin.

Miso: A rich, savoury paste made from fermented soy beans, malt and salt. It is widely used, particularly for miso soup. There are several varieties available; white (or light) miso and red miso are the more common types.

Mochigome: See **Glutinous rice.**

Mochiko: See **Glutinous rice flour.**

Mung bean threads: Known as *saifun* in Japan, these are very fine dried noodles made from mung bean flour. Soak in water for about 10 minutes before use.

Mushrooms, dried: Known as dried *shiitake* in Japan, these mushrooms (*lentinus edodes*) are sold in oriental stores. They are very fragrant, and will keep almost indefinitely in an airtight jar. They have an entirely different flavour from their fresh counterparts. Soak in warm water for 25 to 30 minutes before using. Fresh mushrooms do not make a good substitute.

Napa cabbage: Now widely available in the West, napa cabbage, also known as *hakusai*, celery cabbage, long cabbage or *pe-tsai*, is a cylinder of tightly packed crinkly leaves. It is used in many different types of dish,

10

including stir-fries, salads, casseroles and pickles.

Niboshi: Tiny dried sardines, sometimes used to make *dashi* (q.v.).

Noodles: Japanese noodles come in a variety of types and sizes: *udon* noodles are broad white ribbons made from wheat, *soba* are made from buckwheat, *somen* are very thin wheat noodles and *shirataki* are gelatinous noodles made from yam flour. See also **Mung bean threads** and **Harusame.**

Nori: The dried sheet form of 'laver' seaweed. Nori is used to roll around *sushi* (vinegared rice) and, when cut into slivers, as a garnish. Toast nori before use.

Panko: Coarse breadcrumbs.

Renkon: See **Lotus root.**

Rice cakes: Made by pounding boiled glutinous rice and forming it into small chewy white cakes. They are grilled and eaten with soy sauce, or added to soups.

Rice vinegar: Known as *su* in Japan, this is light, delicately flavoured vinegar, used particularly for making *sushi* (vinegared rice). Rice vinegar is distilled from white rice and is very aromatic. It is much milder than wine or cider vinegar. If unobtainable, substitute distilled white vinegar diluted with water. Seasoned rice vinegars, with sugar and monosodium glutamate added, are also available.

Sake: A rice wine, made by fermenting freshly steamed white rice. Sake is the national drink of Japan. It is also used extensively in cooking. If rice wine is unavailable, a very dry sherry can be substituted.

Sansho powder: A greenish-brown ground spice, made from the pod of the sansho tree. The powder is used in small quantities to season cooked foods.

Sesame: Used as seeds to add flavour and texture (the taste is accentuated if the seeds are dry-fried). Sesame paste or sauce is made by pounding the seeds and is widely available under the name of *tahini*. Sesame seed oil is used for its flavour rather than for cooking, as it burns very easily.

Shichimi pepper: A mixture of seven ingredients — chilli, black pepper, dried orange peel, sesame seeds, poppy seeds, nori seaweed and hemp seeds. They are ground to a spicy hot powder which is often used on noodles.

Shiitake: See **Mushrooms, dried.**

Shirataki: See **Noodles.**

Shiromiso: White soy bean paste.

Shiso leaves: These are used in dishes such as Vegetable Tempura and also as a garnish.

Shoyu: See **Soy sauce.**

Soba: See **Noodles.**

Somen: See **Noodles.**

Soy bean paste: See **Miso, Akamiso** and **Shiromiso.**

Soy sauce: Made from fermented soy beans, soy sauce is used extensively throughout the Orient as a seasoning and condiment. Japanese soy sauce, called *shoyu*, has a completely different flavour from other soy sauces and therefore should always be used in Japanese cooking.

Su: See **Rice vinegar.**

Tofu: See **Bean curd.**

Tonkatsu sauce: A commercially prepared thick brown sauce made from fruit and vegetables combined with spices and seasonings. Soy sauce or ketchup may be used as substitutes.

Transparent noodles: See **Mung bean threads**.
Tsukemono: Japanese pickled vegetables are available ready-made in vacuum packs and jars. They are traditionally served at every Japanese meal.
Udon: See **Noodles**.
Wakame: A young seaweed with long green fronds and smooth texture. It is used in soups and salads.
Wasabi powder: Also known as Japanese horse-radish, this powder is in fact the grated root of a riverside plant. It has a powerful flavour and is traditionally served with raw fish dishes. It is available in tubes or in powder form. Wasabi powder should be mixed with cold water before use.
Water chestnuts: A walnut-size bulb with brown skin. Inside, the flesh is white and crisp. Canned water chestnuts are ready-peeled. Once opened, and with regular changes of water, canned water chestnuts will keep in the refrigerator for up to 2 weeks.

Menus

Breakfast

Boiled Rice
Rolled Rice Wrapped in Nori
Bean Soup
Pressed Salad
Marinated Mackerel
Green Tea

Lunch

Rolled Rice Wrapped in Nori
Chicken Teriyaki
Three-Colour Rice
Egg-battered Sardines
Pressed Salad
Fresh Fruits

Family Dinner

Boiled Rice
Pickled Vegetables
Chicken Cooked with Vegetables
Cod Cooked in Earthenware
Spinach with Bonito Flakes
Bean Soup
Green Tea
Fresh Fruits

Dinner Party

Mackerel Sushi
Thick Egg Soup
Japanese 'Roast' Beef
Vinegared Cucumber
Mixed Vegetables in Tofu Dressing
Boiled Rice
Bean Soup
Fruit Salad
Green Tea

Celebration Meal

Three-Colour Rice
Saffron Soup with Chicken
Japanese Salad
Peach Flowers
Sardine Balls
Fried Tofu Stuffed with Sushi

Note: Adjust quantities of individual dishes according to the number of people being served.

11

Soups & Stocks

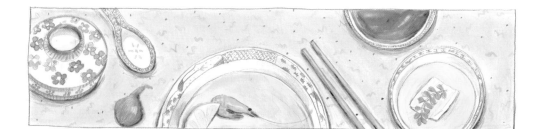

Soup Stock (Dashi) is probably the most essential ingredient in any Japanese kitchen, as it provides the subtle but distinctive flavour so characteristic of Japanese food. It is based on two ingredients — dried fish and dried kelp. Dashi is easy to make, but for the sake of convenience, sachets of instant dashi are available. Almost every Japanese meal includes a soup; indeed most Japanese start the day with a hot and nourishing bowl of Bean Soup (Miso-shiru). There are two main types of soup: clear soups, which are light and delicate; and thick soups, which are almost a meal in themselves and are based on miso (fermented soy bean paste).

Soup Stock

Dashi

25 g (1 oz) konbu (dried kelp)
25g (1 oz) katsuo-bushi (dried bonito flakes)

Put the konbu in a medium saucepan, add 800 ml (1⅓ pints) cold water and leave to soak for about 10 minutes. Place the pan over gentle heat and bring slowly to boiling point. Take out the konbu just before the water boils.

Immediately add the katsuo-bushi and bring to a rapid boil. Boil for a few seconds only, then remove the pan from the heat. Leave to stand for about 1 minute, or until the katsuo-bushi settle down to the bottom. Strain the stock through a clean teatowel into a bowl.
Note: Dashi is an essential flavouring used extensively in Japanese cooking. It is easy to make, requiring only two basic ingredients to give it its characteristic flavour. Instant stock, or *dashi-no-moto*, is available from oriental stores. *Makes 800ml (1⅓ pints)*

Clear Soup with Prawns

Sumashi–jiru

4 headless, uncooked prawns, defrosted if frozen
1 teaspoon salt
a little cornflour for coating
40 g (1½ oz) somen (fine noodles)
600 ml (1 pint) Soup Stock (see left)
½ teaspoon shoyu (Japanese soy sauce)
4 sprigs watercress, trimmed, to garnish

Wash and shell the prawns, retaining the shell on the end of the tail. Remove the black vein from the back of the prawns. Pat dry with a little of the salt, then dust with cornflour. Plunge them into a saucepan of boiling water for 30 seconds, then drain and set aside. Cook the noodles in a saucepan of boiling water for 3 minutes; drain and rinse in cold water, then drain again.

Bring the stock to the boil in a medium-sized saucepan. Season with the shoyu and remaining salt. Divide the prawns and noodles equally between 4 warmed soup bowls and pour over the stock. Garnish with sprigs of watercress and serve.
Note: Uncooked prawns are available (usually frozen) from oriental stores and high-class fishmongers. They are full of flavour, and they look very pretty if the tail shells are left on.

Clear Soup with Prawns; Thick Egg Soup

Thick Egg Soup

Chawan Mushi

100 g (4 oz) boneless chicken breast, skinned
4 teaspoons sake (rice wine)
1½ teaspoons shoyu (Japanese soy sauce)
8 uncooked prawns, defrosted if frozen
salt
4 mangetout
500 ml (18 fl oz) Soup Stock (page 12)
1 teaspoon mirin (sweet rice wine)
3 eggs, beaten
8 small button mushrooms, wiped

Thinly slice the chicken, then sprinkle with 1 teaspoon of the sake and ½ teaspoon of the shoyu. Wash and shell the prawns, taking the black vein out if necessary. Sprinkle the prawns with the remaining sake and a pinch of salt. Plunge the mangetout into a saucepan of lightly salted water for 1 minute, then drain.

Bring the stock to the boil in a medium-sized saucepan. Add ½ teaspoon salt, the mirin and the remaining shoyu. Remove from the heat and leave to cool for 5 minutes, then add the beaten eggs. Divide the chicken equally between 4 Chawan Mushi cups or coffee mugs (see note) and pour in the egg soup. Add 2

mushrooms, 2 prawns and I mangetout to each cup.

Put the cups in a steamer and steam vigorously for 2 minutes. Lower the heat and steam for a further 12 to 14 minutes, or until the juice runs clear when the thickened soup is pierced with a skewer or fork. Alternatively if you do not have a steamer, put the cups or mugs in a shallow baking dish, half-filled with hot water. Cover with foil and cook in a preheated hot oven (220°C/425°F, Gas Mark 7) for 5 minutes, then reduce heat to moderate (180°C/350°F, Gas Mark 4) for 20 to 25 minutes, or until set. Serve the soup immediately. If wished, garnish the cups with extra ingredients, such as prawns, mangetout and mushrooms.

Note: Traditional Chawan Mushi cups are available at Japanese and other oriental stores. They vary in price according to the quality and design of the china, but there are many inexpensive sets to choose from, which look very pretty on the table if you are serving guests. If you do not want to go to the expense of buying them, you can use coffee mugs instead, as long as the circumference of the rim is the same as that of the base, so the soup sets evenly.

Bean Soup

Miso-shiru

25 g (1 oz) niboshi (dried small whole sardines)
1–2 packets wakame (dried young seaweed)
4 tablespoons miso (soy bean paste)
50 g (2 oz) firm tofu (bean curd)
2 spring onions, finely chopped

To make the stock: put the niboshi in a saucepan, add 600 ml (1 pint) water and place over high heat. Bring quickly to the boil and simmer for 5 to 10 minutes, depending on the strength of flavour required. Remove from the heat, strain through a clean teatowel, then return to the rinsed-out pan. Discard the niboshi.

Put the wakame in a bowl and cover with cold water. Leave to soak for 5 to 10 minutes, or until fully expanded; drain and set aside. Put the miso in a small bowl and dilute with a few spoonfuls of the stock. Return the pan of stock to the heat. Just before boiling point is reached, add the diluted miso and lower the heat so that the stock does not boil. Cut the tofu into small cubes and add to the pan with the wakame. Bring to the boil, then remove the soup from the heat and add the finely chopped spring onions. Serve hot, in warmed individual soup bowls.

Note: Miso (soy bean paste) soups are traditional for family meals in Japan, mainly because they are so nutritious and filling.

14

Spring Rain Soup

Harusame Soup

2–3 dried shiitake mushrooms
100 g (4 oz) dehydrated mung bean threads, or harusame (soy bean noodles), soaked in boiling water for 30 minutes
1 litre (1¾ pints) Soup Stock (page 12), or chicken stock
1 tablespoon sake (rice wine)
salt
100 g (4 oz) peeled prawns
6–8 mangetout
1 gobo (burdock root), parboiled (optional)
4–6 spring onions
2 carrots, peeled
few cucumber strips
100 g (4 oz) napa (Chinese cabbage)
few spinach leaves

To garnish:
1 teaspoon grated fresh root ginger
1 spring onion, finely shredded
2 teaspoons puréed daikon (Japanese radish)

Soak the mushrooms in boiling water for 20 minutes. Drain the mung bean threads or harusame and cut into 5 cm (2 inch) lengths. Drain the mushrooms, reserving the liquid, and discard the stems.

Put the stock in a pan. Carefully pour in the reserved mushroom liquid, leaving any sandy sediment at the bottom – this should be discarded. Bring to the boil, then lower the heat and simmer for about 2 minutes. Add the sake and salt to taste.

Divide the stock between 4 warmed individual soup bowls. Arrange the other ingredients attractively on a serving dish, cutting the vegetables to make interesting shapes, if liked. Place the garnish ingredients on separate dishes. Serve immediately.

Note: This light soup has a wonderful aroma and a chewy texture. It can be prepared at the table if wished, in which case each guest has a bowl of stock and adds ingredients to taste.

Saffron Soup with Chicken

Safuran Sumashi

100 g (4 oz) boneless chicken breast, skinned
a little cornflour for coating
600 ml (1 pint) chicken stock
1 whole bone from a flat white fish
pinch of saffron threads
salt
freshly ground black pepper
4 sprigs watercress, trimmed, to garnish

Cut the chicken breast into 2.5 cm (1 inch) squares, then coat lightly with cornflour. Plunge the chicken into a saucepan of boiling water for 5 minutes, or until cooked.

Meanwhile, bring the chicken stock to the boil in a separate saucepan, add the fish bone and boil gently for 5 minutes. Remove the bone and discard. Add the saffron to the stock, with salt and pepper to taste.

Drain the chicken pieces, divide equally between 4 warmed individual soup bowls and pour over the saffron-coloured soup. Garnish with watercress and serve.

Note: The addition of saffron gives this soup a delicate yellow colour which contrasts well with the white of the chicken.

Simple Egg Soup

Kakitama-jiru

1.2 litres (2 pints) Soup Stock (page 12)
2 teaspoons shoyu (Japanese soy sauce)
2 teaspoons cornflour
2 teaspoons salt
2 eggs
1 piece of root ginger, peeled and grated
1 parsley sprig

Bring the stock to the boil in a saucepan. Mix together the shoyu, cornflour and salt and add to the stock. Simmer, stirring, until thickened and smooth.

Beat the eggs until frothy. With a slotted spoon, spread the eggs over the surface of the simmering soup so that they float and do not sink. Add the ginger and parsley before serving.

Spring Rain Soup

Rice & Noodles

Rice is more than just an accompaniment to other dishes: the Japanese consider it to be the most important element of any meal. Sushi dishes, made from Vinegared Rice (Sumeshi), are one of Japan's most popular snacks, although they can also be served as an appetizer or main dish. Sushi are not difficult to prepare at home provided the freshest raw ingredients are used.
Noodles are considered to be country-style fare and are therefore never included in a formal Japanese meal. Nevertheless, noodle dishes of every type are immensely popular, and in Japan there are more noodle bars than any other kind of restaurant.

16

Vinegared Rice

Sumeshi

350 g (12 oz) Japanese short-grain rice
50 ml (2 fl oz) rice vinegar
1½ tablespoons sugar
1 teaspoon salt

Wash the rice very thoroughly, changing the water several times until it is clear. Drain on a bamboo dish or in a very fine sieve for about 1 hour.

When ready to cook, transfer the rice to a deep saucepan (the rice should not fill more than one-quarter of the pan). Add 450 ml (¾ pint) cold water and bring to the boil over high heat. Lower the heat, cover and simmer gently for about 15 minutes, until all the water has been absorbed by the rice. Try not to remove the lid more than once during cooking to check whether the water has been absorbed.

Remove the pan from the heat and leave tightly covered for 10 to 15 minutes. Put the rice vinegar, sugar and salt in a bowl and mix well until the sugar and salt have dissolved.

Transfer the rice to a large (non-metal) bowl and pour over the vinegar mixture. Using a wooden spatula or Japanese rice paddle, fold the vinegar into the rice; do not stir. Leave to cool at room temperature before using in a dish of your choice.

Note: The term *sushi* is a corruption of *sumeshi*, meaning 'vinegared rice', which is used for all Sushi dishes. Rice Balls with Topping (page 18), a small amount of compressed Sumeshi with a piece of raw fish on top, is the most famous of all Sushi. Specially-flavoured rice vinegar is available for making Sumeshi; called Sushi-su, it can be bought in oriental stores.

Fried Rice

Itame Gohan

1 tablespoon vegetable oil
1 medium onion, finely chopped
1 small green pepper, cored, seeded and finely chopped
1 small clove garlic, crushed
575 g (1¼ lb) steamed rice (page 18)
1 egg, beaten
2 tablespoons shoyu (Japanese soy sauce)

Heat the oil in a frying pan. Add the onion, green pepper and garlic and fry until softened. Stir in the rice and heat through, stirring occasionally. Add the egg and shoyu and cook, stirring, for 2 to 3 minutes or until the egg has set. *Serves 6*

Sushi with Five Ingredients

Sushi with Five Ingredients

Gomoku Zushi

1 small mackerel, filleted
salt
rice vinegar
3 dried shiitake mushrooms
1 medium carrot, peeled and shredded
5 tablespoons sugar
3 tablespoons shoyu (Japanese soy sauce)
2 tablespoons mirin (sweet rice wine)
50 g (2 oz) mangetout, cooked
2 eggs
1 tablespoon vegetable oil
Vinegared Rice (see opposite), made with 350 g (12 oz) rice
beni-shoga (pickled ginger roots), shredded
1 sheet nori (dried lava paper) (optional)

Sprinkle the mackerel fillets with salt and leave for 3 to 4 hours. Wash the salt away with rice vinegar. Using your fingers and working from the tail end, remove the transparent skin from each fillet, leaving the silver pattern intact. Remove all the bones which are hidden in the centre of the mackerel fillets. Slice the flesh into thin strips, cover and set aside.

Soak the mushrooms in warm water for 25 minutes, then drain, reserving 120 ml (4 fl oz) of the soaking liquid. Squeeze the mushrooms dry, discard the hard stalks, then finely shred the mushroom caps. Place the mushrooms and carrot in a saucepan with 3 tablespoons of the sugar, the shoyu and mirin. Simmer until all the juice has been absorbed. Cut the mangetout into thin strips.

Beat the eggs in a small bowl, add the remaining sugar and a pinch of salt. Heat the oil in a heavy-based frying pan. Pour in half of the egg mixture, tilting the pan so that it spreads evenly over the base. Fry over the lowest possible heat for 30 seconds, or until the surface of the mixture is dry. Turn the omelette on to a board and leave to cool. Repeat with the remaining mixture, then cut the omelettes into thin strips 5 cm (2 inches) long.

Put the vinegared rice in a large (non-metal) bowl. Add the mushrooms, carrot, mangetout, mackerel and shredded beni-shoga. Using a wooden spatula, gently fold the ingredients into the rice; do not stir. Garnish with the omelette strips. If using nori, grill it under the lowest possible heat for only a second until crisp, then shred into 4 cm (1½ inch) strips with a sharp knife. Arrange the nori shreds on top of the rice before serving. Serve cold.

Note: *Gomoku* means 'five kinds'. Although five kinds of ingredients are sufficient to make this dish, the Japanese do not normally limit themselves to this number. Rice cooked in this way is usually served for a special guest or occasion.

Plain Steamed Rice

Gohan

575 g (1¼ lb) Japanese short- or medium-grain rice
750 ml (1¼ pints) water

Wash the rice thoroughly under cold running water, rubbing it well between the palms of the hands. Drain and repeat this process about 3 times until the running water is clear. Leave to drain in a colander for about 20 minutes.

Put the rice in a heavy pan, add the water, then cover and bring quickly to the boil. Lower the heat and simmer for 20 minutes, by which time most of the water will have been absorbed; do not remove the lid at any stage. Increase the heat and cook for about 20 seconds, then remove the pan from the heat. Leave to stand for 10 minutes, without removing the lid.

Fluff up the rice with a wet rice paddle or a fork. Serve hot in individual rice bowls or on a large serving plate. *Serves 4 to 6*
Note: The Japanese prefer medium- or short-grain rice because it cooks into a fluffy mass that clings together but is not sticky. This type of rice has an entirely different texture from long-grain rice, which has a tendency to be drier with separate grains.

In Japan, a bowl of rice is usually eaten with every meal. It is generally served plain, with the entrée and side dishes. However, there are speciality dishes using rice with various combinations of meat, fish, poultry and vegetables.

The amount of water required to cook the rice will vary according to its origin and the length of time it has been stored since the harvest; the quantity given in this recipe is therefore only an approximate guide. If you are lucky enough to have an electric rice steamer, it will produce perfect rice every time you use it! No salt is added to plain rice in the cooking stage.

Squid Stuffed with Rice

Ika Gohan

175 g (6 oz) glutinous rice
4 small squid, cleaned, with tentacles separated
65 ml (2½ fl oz) shoyu (Japanese soy sauce)
65 ml (2½ fl oz) sake (rice wine)
65 ml (2½ fl oz) mirin (sweet rice wine)
2.5 cm (1 inch) fresh root ginger, peeled and sliced
parsley sprigs, to garnish

Wash the glutinous rice, place in a bowl and cover with water. Leave to soak overnight.

The next day, put the tentacles from the squid in a saucepan with the shoyu, sake and mirin. Bring to the boil, cook for 2 minutes, then remove from the heat. Lift the tentacles out of the liquid with a perforated spoon and chop finely. Reserve the cooking liquid.

Drain the rice, mix with the chopped tentacles, then stuff the squid with this mixture. (Do not over-stuff or the squid may burst during cooking.) Close the squid and secure with toothpicks.

Lay the stuffed squid side by side in a heavy-based saucepan or flameproof casserole. Pour in the reserved cooking liquid from the tentacles, add the sliced ginger and bring to the boil. Cover and simmer for about 40 minutes, or until the squid are tender. Remove from the heat and leave the squid to cool in the sauce.

Cut the squid into rings. Arrange on a large serving platter and garnish with parsley sprigs.
Note: This method of making Ika Gohan is the best, as the rice is cooked inside the squid so that it absorbs the delicious taste of the squid and the simmering sauce.

Squid (also called calamares or inkfish), are becoming widely available from good fishmongers or fish markets. Carefully cooked they are extremely tender.
To prepare squid: wash and skin. Remove the long transparent backbone and clean the inside. Remove the head with its inkbags, and push out the hard core at the centre of the tentacles.

Rice Balls with Topping

Nigiri Zushi

1 tablespoon rice vinegar (approximately)
575 g (1¼ lb) Vinegared Rice (page 16)
about 1 tablespoon wasabi (green horseradish),
mixed to a paste with water
about 30 small slices of raw fresh tuna or sea bass

To serve:
few parsley sprigs
few slices beni-shoga (pickled ginger roots)
shoyu (Japanese soy sauce) to taste

Moisten the hands with a little rice vinegar. Scoop up 2 tablespoons rice in one hand then, with the other hand, squeeze the rice into an egg oval, about 5 cm (2 inches) long. Dab the top with wasabi paste, then cover with a slice of fish, pressing it down firmly. Repeat with the remaining rice, wasabi paste and fish, to make about 30 rice ovals.

Arrange the rice ovals on a tray and garnish with the parsley and beni-shoga. Hand shoyu separately as a dip for the fish. Serve cold with plenty of green tea. *Makes about 30*
Note: This is the Japanese snack which is prepared at the popular sushi bars. The tuna or sea bass topping given here can be replaced with shrimps. These should be peeled, deveined and boiled briefly, with a toothpick inserted along the underside to prevent them curling. Cut them in half, keeping the back side intact, then place on top of the wasabi.

Another variation is to serve the rice ovals topped with rectangular pieces of thin omelette. These make marvellous hors d'oeuvre.

Mackerel Sushi

Saba Zushi

1 large fresh mackerel, filleted
salt
rice vinegar
Vinegared Rice (page 16), made with 350 g (12 oz)
rice and 450 ml (¾ pint) water

To garnish:
beni-shoga (pickled ginger roots)
shredded chives

Put the mackerel fillets on a bed of salt, then pour over more salt to completely cover the fish. Leave for several hours or overnight. Remove the fillets from the salt and rub the salt off roughly with paper towels. Wash the remaining salt away with rice vinegar. Using your fingers and working from the tail end, remove the transparent skin from each fillet, leaving the silver pattern intact. Carefully remove all the bones which are hidden in the mackerel fillets.

Put the mackerel fillets, skin side down, on a board. Slice off the thick flesh from the centre to make the fillets even in thickness. Reserve these slices of flesh.

Place one of the mackerel fillets, skin side down, on the bottom of a wooden mould, or a loaf tin lined with a large sheet of cling film. Fill any gaps with some of the reserved slices of thick flesh. Press the vinegared rice down firmly on top of the fish with your hands. Top with the remaining mackerel fillet, skin side up, and fill in any gaps with the remaining slice of thick flesh. Place the wooden lid on top of the mould (or wrap in the sheet of cling film) and put a weight on top. Leave the mackerel sushi wrapped in cling film in a cool place (not the refrigerator) for a few hours or overnight. Remove from the mould or tin, unwrap and slice into bite-sized pieces. Garnish with beni-shoga and chives, and serve cold.

Note: This combination of fresh mackerel and vinegared rice is well worth the time and effort it takes to prepare. Special wooden moulds can be purchased for preparing Saba Zushi, although a loaf tin lined with cling film can be used successfully. Saba Zushi makes a popular party starter or pre-dinner appetizer.

Mackerel Sushi; Three-Colour Rice (page 22)

Rolled Rice Wrapped in Nori

Nori-maki

25 g (1 oz) packet kanpyo (dried shaved gourd
strings), cut into 15 cm (6 inch) lengths
salt
6 tablespoons sugar
6 tablespoons shoyu (Japanese soy sauce)
5–6 sheets of nori (dried lava paper)
3 dried shiitake mushrooms
1 medium carrot, peeled and shredded
2 tablespoons mirin (sweet rice wine)
100 g (4 oz) fresh spinach leaves, washed and
trimmed
Vinegared Rice (page 16), made with 500g
(1 lb 2 oz) rice and 685 ml (23 fl oz) water
beni-shoga (pickled ginger roots), shredded, to
garnish (optional)

Thick egg omelette:
2 eggs
3 tablespoons Soup Stock (page 12)
2 tablespoons sugar
1 tablespoon vegetable oil

Fish flakes:
1 white fish fillet (e.g. cod, haddock or whiting)
1½ tablespoons sake (rice wine)
1½ tablespoons sugar
red food colouring

Put the kanpyo in a saucepan, add 1 teaspoon salt and a few drops of water, then squeeze with your fingers. Rinse the salt away, then add enough water to cover and soak for 20 minutes. Place the pan over heat and boil until the kanpyo becomes soft enough to break if pinched between the fingers, then drain. Add half of the sugar and shoyu, then simmer until all the juice disappears. Remove from the heat and set aside.

Grill the nori sheets lightly on both sides, placing them on the lowest possible grill position. This brings out their flavour and makes them crisp. Remove from the heat and set aside.

Make the omelette: beat the eggs in a bowl, add the stock, sugar and ¼ teaspoon salt and beat well to mix. Heat the oil in a heavy-based (preferably square) frying pan. Pour in one-third of the egg mixture, cook until it is set, then fold in half. Grease the empty half of the pan with a wad of paper towels dipped in oil. Pour the remaining egg mixture into the empty half of the pan and cook until set. Fold on to the previously cooked half, then remove this omelette 'sandwich' from the pan. Leave to cool, then cut into long strips about 5mm (¼ inch) thick.

Make the fish flakes: put the fish fillet in a saucepan, add just enough water to cover and bring to the boil. Drain thoroughly. Using 2 pairs of hashi (chopsticks) or a fork, mash the fish to make flakes. Put the sake in a shallow frying pan with the sugar, ¼ teaspoon salt and enough food colouring diluted with a little water to turn the mixture pink. Add the fish flakes, place over very low heat and cook for 2 minutes, stirring all the time. Remove from the heat and leave to cool

Soak the mushrooms in warm water for 25 minutes, then drain and reserve 120 ml (4 fl oz) of the soaking liquid. Squeeze the mushrooms dry, discard the hard stalks, and finely shred the mushroom caps. Place the mushrooms and carrot in a saucepan with the remaining sugar and shoyu, the mirin and the reserved soaking liquid from the mushrooms. Simmer over very low heat until all the juice has been absorbed.

Blanch the spinach in lightly salted water for 1 minute. Drain, then squeeze out the water with your hands.

Place a sheet of nori, shortest side closest to you, on a makisu (bamboo mat). Put half a sheet of nori crossways in the centre on top (this is not strictly necessary, but it does help to prevent the wrapper splitting). Spread 200–225 g (7–8 oz) vinegared rice over the nori, leaving a 1 cm (½ inch) margin on the side nearest to you and on the opposite side. Using your fingers, press the rice to the nori. Place one-quarter of the kanpyo and one-third of the omelette strips, fish flakes, mushrooms, carrots and spinach crossways to within 5 cm (2 inches) of the side furthest from you. Roll up the makisu from the side nearest to you so that the ingredients are in the centre of the vinegared rice. Lightly press the rolled makisu with your fingers. Repeat with more nori and the same filling ingredients to make 3 thick nori-maki altogether.

Use the remaining vinegared rice, kanpyo and nori to make thinner nori-maki: place half a sheet of nori on a makisu, with the longest side nearest to you. Put a handful of rice on the nori, then spread it with your fingers and press it to the nori, leaving a 5mm (¼ inch) margin on the side nearest to you and 1 cm (½ inch) on the opposite side. Put 1–2 kanpyo strips crossways in the centre and roll the makisu from the side nearest to you.

To serve: cut the thick nori-maki into 6–8 rings and the thinner ones into 4–6 pieces. Arrange them on a wooden or bamboo dish, or on a serving platter, then garnish with shredded beni-shoga. Serve cold.
Note: In this recipe, Sumeshi (vinegared rice) is mixed with kanpyo omelette strips, fish flakes, mushrooms, carrots and spinach to make Nori-maki (*maki* means 'rolling'). You can use almost any ingredient you wish as long as it looks attractive: any colour goes well with the brilliant white of Sumeshi. Strips of cucumber look good, or strips of raw tuna, smoked cod's roe, ham, cheese and tsuke-mono (Japanese pickled vegetables); you can even use canned sardines, tuna, salmon or anchovies.

Rolled Rice Wrapped in Nori

Three-Colour Rice

Sanshoku Gohan

500 g (1 lb 2oz) Japanese short-grain rice
fish flakes as for Rice Wrapped in Nori (page 20)

Meat flakes:
2 tablespoons shoyu (Japanese soy sauce)
2 tablespoons Soup Stock (page 12)
1½ tablespoons sugar
1 tablespoon sake (rice wine)
1 tablespoon mirin (sweet rice wine)
1 teaspoon finely chopped fresh root ginger
225 g (8 oz) minced chicken or beef

Egg flakes:
4 eggs
1½ tablespoons sugar
1 tablespoon sake (rice wine)
1 tablespoon vegetable oil
½ teaspoon shoyu (Japanese soy sauce)
⅓ teaspoon salt

To garnish:
4 large, unpeeled, cooked prawns
6 mangetout, cooked and halved
lemon slices

Make plain boiled rice as for Vinegared Rice (page 16), using 685 ml (23 fl oz) water.

Make the meat flakes: put all the ingredients, except the meat, in a saucepan and bring to the boil. Add the meat and stir well. Cook over low heat, stirring all the time, until all the juice has been absorbed. Remove from the heat, cover and keep warm.

Make the egg flakes: beat the eggs in a saucepan, add the remaining ingredients and cook over moderate heat, stirring all the time, until the eggs are very finely scrambled. Remove from the heat and stir for 30 seconds.

Put the hot rice in 3 individual bowls and garnish with the fish, meat and egg flakes, prawns, mangetout halves and lemon slices. Serve warm.

Note: Sanshoku Gohan is a typical lunch dish, especially enjoyed by Japanese school children. It is traditionally made as a portable lunch to be carried in a beautiful lacquered box.

Rice with Cockles

Asari Gohan

500 g (1 lb 2 oz) Japanese short-grain rice
225 g (8 oz) cockles
salt
5 cm (2 inch) piece fresh root ginger
3 tablespoons shoyu (Japanese soy sauce)
2 tablespoons mirin (sweet rice wine)
1 tablespoon sake (rice wine)
2 tablespoons sugar

Make plain boiled rice as for Vinegared Rice (page 16), using 685 ml (23 fl oz) water.

Wash the cockles in salted water and drain. Peel and slice the ginger. Put the shoyu, mirin, sake and sugar in a saucepan and bring to the boil. Add the cockles and ginger slices, bring back to the boil, then lower the heat. Skim, then cook gently until all the juice has soaked into the cockles.

Divide the hot rice equally between 4 individual noodle bowls, arrange the cooked cockles on top and serve immediately.

Note: This dish is served at lunchtime. Most Japanese homes have cooked rice keeping warm in an electric rice cooker from morning to night. For lunch, a little rice is used with whatever fresh ingredient is available on the day.

Parent-Child Bowl

Oyako Donburi

500 g (1 lb 2 oz) Japanese short-grain rice
2 medium onions
4 spring onions
225 g (8 oz) boneless chicken breast meat, skinned
400 ml (14 fl oz) Soup Stock (page 12)
5 tablespoons shoyu (Japanese soy sauce)
2 tablespoons sake (rice wine)
1 tablespoon mirin (sweet rice wine)
1 tablespoon sugar
4 eggs, beaten
watercress, roughly chopped, to garnish

Make plain boiled rice as for Vinegared Rice (page 16), using 685 ml (23 fl oz) water. Slice the onions thinly. Cut the spring onions in half lengthways, reserve the green part, then slice the remainder into 5 cm (2 inch) lengths. Chop the chicken into bite-sized pieces. Mix the stock with the shoyu, sake, mirin and sugar and stir well.

Pour one-quarter of the stock mixture into a small, heavy-based frying pan or pancake pan. Add one-quarter of the thinly sliced onions and bring to the boil, then add one-quarter of the chicken meat and cook for 2 minutes. Add one-quarter of the spring onions, cook for a few seconds, then pour over one-quarter of the beaten eggs. Cook until only just set.

Remove the pan from the heat, sprinkle over a little chopped watercress, then remove from the pan. Repeat with the remaining ingredients to make 4 parent-child bowls altogether. Divide the hot rice equally between 4 individual plates, top with the chicken and egg mixture, and garnish with the reserved spring onion and the remaining watercress.

Note: Parent-child bowl is a direct translation of *oyako*, and the dish is so named because the recipe combines both chicken and egg. *Donburi* often refers to a large bowl of rice topped with poultry, meat or fish. In Japan a special Oyako Donburi frying pan is used but a pancake pan can be used successfully.

22

Fried Tofu Stuffed with Sushi

Inari Zushi

350 g (12 oz) Japanese short-grain rice
1½ tablespoons mirin (sweet rice wine)
20 g (¾ oz) kanpyo (dried shaved gourd strings)
salt
135 ml (4½ fl oz) Soup Stock (page 12)
1½ tablespoons shoyu (Japanese soy sauce)
4 teaspoons sugar
50 ml (2 fl oz) rice vinegar
50 g (2 oz) tsukemono (pickled vegetables), finely chopped
10 pieces abur-age (deep-fried bean curd)
bamboo leaves, to serve

Wash the rice in at least 3 changes of water, until the water becomes clear. Drain well, then place in a large saucepan. Pour in 400 ml (14 fl oz) fresh cold water and leave the rice to soak for 2 hours.

Add the mirin to the pan, cover with the lid and place over high heat. Bring to the boil then simmer for 10 to 15 minutes, until all the water has been absorbed. Remove from the heat and leave to stand, covered, for 15 minutes.

Wet the kanpyo a little and, using your hands, rub it with a lot of salt. Wash well to remove the surface salt, then place the kanpyo in a small saucepan, cover with cold water and bring to the boil. Simmer for 5 minutes until the kanpyo becomes soft, then drain off the water. Add the stock to the kanpyo together with the shoyu and half of the sugar. Simmer gently for a further 5 minutes, then remove from the heat and set aside.

Turn the cooked rice into a large bowl. Mix together the rice vinegar, remaining sugar and ⅔ teaspoon salt. Add the tsukemono and fold into the rice with a wooden rice paddle or spatula; do not stir.

Cut each piece of abur-age in half and open up with your fingers to make a pocket. Stuff the pockets with the rice mixture until two-thirds full.

Tie each pocket with a 15 cm (6 inch) string of cooked kanpyo. Arrange on a bed of bamboo leaves and serve. *Serves 4 to 6*

Note: To make this dish look more attractive, turn half of the abur-age (fried bean curd) inside out after cutting them in half. The texture of the outside is like smooth leather, whereas the inside looks like a sponge, which gives an interesting contrast in both colour and texture. Bamboo leaves can be bought at some oriental shops; if you cannot obtain them, use any other long green leaves instead, such as Cos lettuce.

Parent-Child Bowl; Noodles in Egg Soup (page 24)

Noodles with Broth

Tsukimi Udon

500 g (1 lb) udon (thick dried noodles)
900 ml (1½ pints) Soup Stock (page 12)
1 tablespoon sugar
1½ teaspoons salt
1 tablespoon shoyu (Japanese soy sauce)
4 eggs

To garnish:
2 spring onions, thinly sliced
13 cm (5 inch) square piece of nori (dried lava paper), toasted and finely shredded

Add the noodles to a large pan of boiling water, stirring constantly. Bring back to the boil, then add 250 ml (8 fl oz) cold water. Bring back to the boil again, then cook the noodles for 10 to 12 minutes until *al dente*. Drain, then rinse under cold running water and drain again.

Put the stock, sugar, salt and shoyu in a large pan and stir well. Bring to the boil over high heat, then add the noodles. Bring back to the boil, stirring constantly, then cook until the noodles are heated through.

Pour into warmed individual bowls, then break 1 egg over each bowl. Cover the bowls with lids and the heat from the noodles will cook the eggs. Garnish with spring onions and nori shreds. Serve hot.

Note: Noodles are consumed in large quantities, and with great relish, in Japan. 'Slurping' is good etiquette and everyone eats noodles with their meals or as a snack. There are many varieties of noodle in Japan – thick and wide ones, coloured ones and ones made from buckwheat. This recipe uses the traditional thick, wide udon, and the egg on top is like a full moon – the title literally translated means 'seeing the moon noodles'.

Noodles in Egg Soup

Kakitama Udon

500 g (1 lb) udon (thick dried noodles)
salt
1 litre (1¾ pints) Soup Stock (page 12)
50 ml (2 fl oz) shoyu (Japanese soy sauce)
2 tablespoons mirin (sweet rice wine)
3 tablespoons cornflour
4 eggs, beaten

To serve:
3 spring onions, finely chopped
2.5 cm (1 inch) piece fresh root ginger, peeled and grated
shichimi pepper

Plunge the udon into a large saucepan of lightly salted boiling water. Bring back to the boil, then lower the heat and simmer, uncovered, for about 10 minutes until they are soft but not soggy. Drain well in a colander and rinse under cold running water, to remove excess starch.

Bring the stock to the boil in a saucepan with the shoyu, mirin and ½ teaspoon salt. Mix the cornflour to a smooth paste with a little water, add to the pan and stir until the soup thickens slightly. Slowly add the eggs to the soup, then cook over low heat until threads of egg float to the surface. Remove the pan from the heat.

Put the cooked udon in a bowl of hot water for a few seconds to reheat them. Drain, then divide equally between 4 individual noodle bowls. Pour the egg soup over the noodles, then sprinkle over the spring onions. Place a little grated ginger in a small dish. Serve hot, with shichimi pepper and ginger handed separately.

Chilled Noodles

Hiyashi Somen

500 g (1 lb) somen (fine dried noodles)
8–12 large, headless, uncooked prawns, defrosted if frozen
4–5 dried shiitake mushrooms
2 tablespoons shoyu (Japanese soy sauce)
2 tablespoons mirin (sweet rice wine)
1 tablespoon sugar
2 small tomatoes, quartered, to garnish
225 g (8 oz) boiled ham, finely shredded
½ cucumber, finely shredded
2.5 cm (1 inch) piece fresh root ginger, peeled and grated
2 shiso leaves or spring onions, finely chopped

Sauce:
15 cm (6 inch) square konbu (dried kelp)
25 g (1 oz) katsuo-bushi (dried bonito flakes)
65 ml (2½ fl oz) shoyu (Japanese soy sauce)
65 ml (2½ fl oz) mirin (sweet rice wine)

Plunge the somen into a large saucepan of boiling water. Cook, uncovered, over moderate heat for 8 to 10 minutes until the somen are tender but still crisp. Drain in a colander and rinse under cold running water to remove excess starch.

Place the somen in a large glass bowl and cover with fresh cold water. Add a few ice cubes, then place the bowl in the refrigerator while preparing the remaining ingredients.

Wash and shell the prawns, retaining the shell on the end of the tail. Remove the black vein from the back of the prawns. Plunge the prawns into a saucepan of boiling water for 2 minutes, then drain thoroughly and rinse under cold running water until cool. Drain on paper towels and chill in the refrigerator until serving time.

Soak the mushrooms in warm water for 25 minutes, then drain and reserve 300 ml (½ pint) of the soaking liquid (if there is not enough, make up the quantity with water). Squeeze the mushrooms dry, discard the hard stalks, then shred the caps finely. Place them in a saucepan with the shoyu, mirin and sugar and cook until all the liquid has been absorbed. Remove from the heat and set aside.

To make the sauce: pour the reserved soaking liquid from the mushrooms into a saucepan. Add the konbu, katsuo-bushi, shoyu and mirin and bring to the boil,

Steamed Pink Rice with Beans; Chilled Noodles; Noodles with Broth

taking out the konbu just before boiling. Cook for 5 minutes, then strain through a fine sieve lined with muslin or cheesecloth. Leave the sauce to cool, then chill in the refrigerator.

To serve: garnish the somen in cold water with quartered tomatoes. Arrange the ham, cucumber, mushrooms and chilled prawns in a serving dish. Divide the cold sauce equally between 4 individual bowls and stir in the grated ginger and chopped shiso leaves or spring onions. Each diner puts a little of the ham, cucumber, mushrooms and prawns into his or her bowl of sauce, then takes some cold somen with hashi (chopsticks) and dips this into the sauce before eating. **Note:** This is very popular in the summer in Japan as it is a cooling meal to serve during the long and stifling months of hot weather.

Steamed Pink Rice with Beans

Sekihan

200 g (7 oz) azuki beans
750 g (1¾ lb) glutinous rice
goma jio (salted sesame seeds), made with 1
teaspoon black sesame seeds and 2 teaspoons salt

Pick over and wash the azuki, then put them in a pan and cover with water. Bring to the boil, then drain; cover with fresh cold water and bring to the boil again. Lower the heat, cover with a lid and simmer gently for about 40 minutes, adding more water to keep the beans covered during cooking. Drain and reserve the cooking liquid.

Wash the rice thoroughly; drain and place in a bowl. Cover with the reserved azuki liquid and leave to stand overnight to allow the rice to acquire a pinkish colour.

Drain the rice and reserve the liquid. Mix the rice and azuki together, taking care not to crush the beans. Line a steamer plate, or other heatproof plate, with a piece of cheesecloth. Bring the water in the steamer to the boil, then spread the rice and bean mixture on the cloth, patting it smooth and making a few vent holes in it. Steam over high heat for about 50 minutes until the rice is cooked, basting every 12 minutes with the reserved azuki liquid.

Divide between warmed individual serving bowls and sprinkle with goma jio. Serve hot or at room temperature. *Serves 8 to 10*
Note: This pale pink rice is a celebration dish, prepared for special occasions such as birthdays. For the rice to acquire a pink colour, preparation must be started the day before the dish is required.

Vegetables

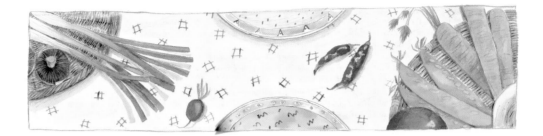

There is an enormous variety of vegetables available in Japan.
Although some of them cannot be found in the West, many kinds are
available canned or dried. Oriental stores stock some of the more
unusual varieties, such as burdock and daikon.
Daikon is often cooked, but it is particularly popular shredded raw
and used as an attractive garnish. Mushrooms are also popular –
especially the shiitake mushroom which imparts a strong flavour
and has an appealing texture. Vegetables are often salted and
parboiled even when used in salads, as in Vinegared Cucumber
(Sunomono), the traditional vinegared salad.

Mixed Vegetables in Tofu Dressing

Yasai No Aemono

3 dried shiitake mushrooms
½ cake kon-nyaku (arum root)
15–25 g (½–1 oz) abur-age (deep-fried bean curd),
or 2 slices boiled ham
1 small carrot, peeled
50 g (2 oz) French beans, topped and tailed
400 ml (14 fl oz) Soup Stock (page 12)
1 tablespoon shoyu (Japanese soy sauce)
2 teaspoons sugar

Dressing:
100 g (4 oz) silken tofu (bean curd)
4 tablespoons sesame seeds, toasted and pounded,
or 2 tablespoons sesame paste (tahini)
2½ tablespoons sugar
1 teaspoon salt

Soak the mushrooms in warm water for 20 to 25
minutes, then drain. Squeeze the mushrooms dry,
discard the hard stalks, then cut the caps into thin strips.
Cut the kon-nyaku into strips about 4 cm (1½ inches)
long and 5 mm (¼ inch) thick. Blanch in boiling water for
a few seconds. If using abur-age, place in a bowl and
pour over boiling water to cover. Drain and cut into
strips 5 mm (¼ inch) wide. Cut the ham (if using) and the
carrot and French beans into strips about the same size
as the abur-age.

Bring the stock to the boil in a saucepan with the
shoyu and sugar. Add the prepared ingredients (except
the ham, if used) and simmer gently for 10 minutes.
Remove from the heat and leave to cool.

Meanwhile, make the dressing: drop the tofu into a
saucepan of boiling water, bring back to the boil, then
drain. Put the tofu on a board, place a flat plate or
another board on top and press down to squeeze out
excess moisture.

Force the tofu through a sieve into a bowl, pressing
it with a wooden spatula. Add the sesame paste, sugar
and salt and mix well. Drain the cooled vegetables,
reserving the juice. Add the vegetables to the dressing,
with the ham, if used. Mix well, adding a little of the
reserved juice from the vegetables if the dressing is too
thick. Transfer to a salad bowl and serve cold.

Note: Vegetables are rarely used raw in Japan, but are
often part-cooked in a little stock. The toasted sesame
seeds give the creamy tofu dressing a 'nutty' flavour.

Mixed Vegetables in Tofu Dressing; Japanese Salad

Japanese Salad

Wafu Salad

½ medium carrot, peeled
1 cucumber
½ bunch spring onions
100 g (4 oz) boneless chicken breast meat
1 tablespoon sake (rice wine)
15 g (½ oz) wakame (dried young seaweed)
shiso or lettuce leaves, to serve

Gomadare dressing:
4 tablespoons sesame seeds, toasted and pounded,
or 2 tablespoons sesame paste (tahini)
1 small garlic clove, peeled and grated
5 tablespoons rice vinegar
3 tablespoons Soup Stock (page 12)
1 tablespoon shoyu (Japanese soy sauce)
1 tablespoon mayonnaise
pinch of chilli powder
1 teaspoon salt

First make the gomadare dressing: mix all the ingredients together in a bowl with the salt. Set aside.
Finely shred the carrot, cucumber and spring onions and place them in separate bowls of ice-cold water to crisp up, while preparing the remaining ingredients.
Skin the chicken and lay on a plate, sprinkle with sake and a little salt, then place in a steamer and steam for 12 minutes or until tender. Remove from the steamer and leave to cool. When cool, shred the chicken finely with your fingers and return to the juices on the plate.
Put the wakame in a bowl and cover with cold water. Leave to soak for 5 to 10 minutes, or until it becomes fully expanded and soft. Drain in a sieve, rinse with boiling water, then rinse under cold running water. Drain well and squeeze out any excess water with your hands. Cut the wakame into 2.5 cm (1 inch) lengths if it is not already chopped.
Line a large plate with shiso or lettuce leaves. Place the bowl of gomadare dressing in the centre and arrange all the shredded ingredients around it.
Note: The key to making this salad look authentic is to shred the vegetables as thin as a needle.

Hot Daikon with Sauce

Soboro Ankake

1 large daikon (Japanese radish)
salt
400 ml (14 fl oz) Soup Stock (page 12)
2 tablespoons shoyu (Japanese soy sauce)
4 teaspoons mirin (sweet rice wine)
1 tablespoon vegetable oil
100 g (4 oz) minced beef
1 teaspoon sugar
1½ tablespoons cornflour

Peel the daikon and cut into rounds about 4 cm (1½ inches) thick. Plunge into a saucepan of simmering, lightly salted water, then cover with an otoshi-buta (small wooden lid) or small upturned plate and cook very gently for about 45 minutes. Drain and set aside.

Pour the stock into the rinsed-out pan, then add half of the shoyu, 1 teaspoon of the mirin and ½ teaspoon salt. Bring to the boil, add the drained daikon and cover with an otoshi-buta or a sheet of greaseproof paper (the plate would be too heavy at this stage). Simmer over very low heat for a further 30 minutes, then remove from the heat and keep warm.

Heat the oil in a separate saucepan, add the minced beef and fry until it changes colour, stirring all the time to remove any lumps. Add the remaining shoyu and mirin, the sugar and salt to taste. Pour in the liquid from the daikon, cook over high heat for 2 minutes, then taste and adjust seasoning – it should be slightly salty. Mix the cornflour to a smooth paste with 3 tablespoons cold water. Add to the pan of meat and stir until the mixture thickens. Arrange 2 daikon pieces in each of 4 warmed individual bowls and pour the meat sauce over them. Serve hot.
Note: Daikon is usually associated with salads or garnishes, when it is grated or cut into shapes. In this recipe the daikon is cooked slowly over low heat to make a warming winter dish, but it still retains its characteristic crispness.

Vinegared Cucumber

Sunomono

1 large or 2 small cucumbers
1 teaspoon salt
15 g (½ oz) wakame (dried young seaweed)
2.5–4 cm (1–1½ inch) piece fresh root ginger

Saubaizu sauce:
3 tablespoons rice vinegar
1 tablespoon shoyu (Japanese soy sauce)
1 tablespoon sugar
¼–½ teaspoon salt

Halve the cucumber(s) lengthways; remove the seeds with a sharp-edged teaspoon. Slice the cucumber very thinly and sprinkle with the salt. Using your hands, squeeze the cucumber slices a few times, then rinse under cold running water in a bamboo strainer or sieve.

Put the wakame in a bowl and cover with cold water. Leave to soak for 5 to 10 minutes, or until it becomes fully expanded and soft. Drain in a sieve, rinse with boiling water, then rinse under cold running water. Drain well and squeeze out any excess water with your hands. Cut the wakame into 2.5 cm (1 inch) lengths, if it is not already chopped.

Peel and shred the ginger, then place in a bowl of ice-cold water to crisp up. Put all the ingredients for the sauce in a bowl, mix well together, then add the sliced cucumber and wakame. Toss well.

Transfer the salad to individual salad bowls, shaping it into neat mounds. Drain the shredded ginger and sprinkle over the top. Serve cold.
Note: This classic Japanese vinegared salad of finely sliced cucumber and soft wakame can be served as an hors d'oeuvre or as a refreshing accompaniment to a main meal.

Spring Onions with Mustard Miso Sauce

Negi no Karashiae

2 bunches thin spring onions
15 g (½ oz) wakame (dried young seaweed)

Mustard miso sauce:
3 tablespoons shiromiso (white soy bean paste)
3 tablespoons sugar
1 teaspoon Japanese or other hot mustard
1 teaspoon shoyu (Japanese soy sauce)
1 teaspoon mirin (sweet rice wine)

Trim the spring onions, then plunge into a saucepan of boiling water for 2 minutes. Drain in a colander and hold under cold running water until cool. Drain thoroughly.

Hold 2 spring onions together side by side and fold them 3 to 4 times, until about 4 cm (1½ inches) long. Tie each pair together at the centre, using the soft green part.

Put the wakame in a bowl and cover with cold water. Leave to soak for 5 to 10 minutes, or until it becomes fully expanded and soft. Drain in a sieve, rinse with boiling water, then rinse under cold running water. Drain well and squeeze out any excess water. Cut the wakame into 2.5 cm (1 inch) lengths, if it is not already chopped.

Place the wakame on a large serving plate, then arrange the spring onion bunches on top. Put all the ingredients for the mustard miso sauce in a small bowl and stir well to mix. Pour the sauce over the vegetables and serve immediately.
Note: Mustard miso sauce is a very traditional Japanese dressing, which complements the strong taste of the spring onions used in this recipe. When spring onions are not in season, use another vegetable such as lightly cooked leeks or fennel.

Vegetable Tempura

Kaki-age

½ medium carrot
50 g (2 oz) French beans
2 potatoes, peeled
1 egg
50 g (2 oz) plain flour, plus extra for sprinkling
vegetable oil for deep-frying

To serve:
Tentsuyu sauce as for Deep-fried Fish and
Vegetables (page 54)
2.5 cm (1 inch) piece fresh root ginger, peeled and
grated
5 cm (2 inch) piece daikon (Japanese radish), peeled
and grated

Peel the carrot and shred finely into 5cm (2 inch) lengths. Slice the French beans in half lengthways, then cut into 5 cm (2 inch) lengths. Cut the potatoes into matchsticks.

Put the egg in a bowl, stir in 50 ml (2 fl oz) ice-cold water, then sift in the 50 g (2 oz) flour. Using 2 pairs of hashi (chopsticks) or 2 forks, mix to a lumpy batter.

Put some of the prepared vegetables in a ladle and sprinkle them with a little flour. Add 1 or 2 tablespoons of the batter and mix well in the ladle.

Heat the oil in a deep-fat frier or deep frying pan to about 160°C/325°F. Deep-fry the vegetables, a ladleful at a time, for about 2 minutes until they are golden and crisp. Remove from the hot oil with a perforated spoon and drain on paper towels.

To serve: pour the tentsuyu sauce into 4 small bowls. Put the grated ginger and daikon in separate bowls. Fold a large paper towel in half and place on a bamboo dish or serving platter. Arrange the vegetables on the paper and serve immediately, with the bowls of sauce, ginger and daikon. Each diner should mix grated ginger and daikon to taste with some of the sauce, then dip the vegetables into the sauce before eating.

Note: Kaki-age is often made with leftover batter from Tempura (Deep-fried Fish and Vegetables) (page 54). The trimmings from the fish are sometimes mixed with the vegetables and deep-fried in the batter.

Vegetable Tempura

Vegetable, Noodle and Sesame Salad

Gomadare Salad

4 dried shiitake mushrooms
350 g (12 oz) daikon (Japanese radish), thinly sliced
salt
100 g (4 oz) carrots, thinly sliced
1 abur-age (deep-fried bean curd)
1 packet of shirataki (yam noodles)
4 tablespoons Soup Stock (page 12)
1 tablespoon sugar
1 tablespoon shoyu (Japanese soy sauce)

Dressing:
3 tablespoons white sesame seeds, toasted
2 tablespoons vinegar
2 tablespoons sugar
1 tablespoon shoyu (Japanese soy sauce)
1½ teaspoons salt

Soak the mushrooms in water for 30 minutes. Drain and discard the hard stalks. Sprinkle the daikon with salt. Sprinkle the carrots with salt.

Place the abur-age, shirataki and mushrooms in a saucepan and add the stock, sugar and shoyu. Bring to the boil and simmer until the noodles are tender.

Meanwhile drop the daikon and carrots into a pan of boiling water and simmer until just tender. Drain well and cool.

Allow the noodle mixture to cool, then add the daikon and carrots and mix together.

To make the dressing, pound the sesame seeds in a mortar with a pestle. Add the remaining dressing ingredients and mix well. Pour the dressing over the salad and toss to coat.

Tofu in Dashi Sauce

Agedashi Dofu

225 g (8 oz) silken or firm tofu (bean curd)
cornflour for coating
vegetable oil for deep-frying

Dashi sauce:
200 ml (7 fl oz) Soup Stock (page 12)
4 tablespoons mirin (sweet rice wine)
4 tablespoons shoyu (Japanese soy sauce)

To serve:
5 cm (2 inch) piece daikon (Japanese radish), peeled and grated
4 shiso or lettuce leaves, finely shredded

If using silken tofu (bean curd), drop the pieces into a saucepan of boiling water for 1 minute to make them firm. Drain well, then cut the tofu into 6–8 squares. Roll each piece in cornflour until evenly coated, shaking off any excess.

Heat the oil in a deep-fat frier or deep frying pan to 160°C/325°F, add the tofu and deep-fry until golden brown. Remove from the oil with a perforated spoon and drain on paper towels.

To make the sauce: pour the stock into a saucepan, add the mirin and shoyu, and bring to the boil. Divide the sauce equally between 4 warmed individual bowls. Place 3–4 pieces of fried tofu in each bowl, then garnish with grated daikon and shredded shiso or lettuce leaves. Serve immediately.

Note: If using Japanese silken tofu (bean curd), it is essential to boil it before frying, as this makes it firmer. Chinese tofu is already firm and does not need to be boiled first.

Simmered Soy Beans

Nimame

200 g (7 oz) soy beans
salt
1 × 250 g (5 oz) can renkon (lotus root) or water chestnuts, drained (optional)
1 × 200 g (7 oz) can gobo (burdock root), drained
½ medium carrot, peeled
½ cake kon-nyaku (arum root)
10 cm (4 inch) square konbu (dried kelp)
25 g (1 oz) sugar
5 tablespoons shoyu (Japanese soy sauce)

Wash the soy beans, then place in a bowl and cover with lightly salted water, allowing 3 times as much water as the volume of soya beans. Leave to soak overnight.

Put the beans and their soaking liquid in a saucepan and bring to the boil. Add 200 ml (7 fl oz) cold water, place an otoshi-buta (small wooden lid) or upturned plate directly on top of the beans and cover with a lid. Simmer for about 1 hour, or until the beans become soft.

Meanwhile cut the renkon or water chestnuts (if using) and the gobo into small cubes, about 1 cm (½ inch) square. Cut the carrot into 1 cm (½ inch) squares. Tear the kon-nyaku into similar-sized pieces with your hands. Cut the konbu into 1 cm (½ inch) squares.

When the beans are cooked, add the renkon or water chestnuts, the drained gobo and the kon-nyaku. Cover again with the otoshi-buta or plate and simmer for about 10 minutes until the gobo is cooked. Add the squares of carrot and konbu and half of the sugar. Continue cooking for a further 10 minutes until the carrots are tender, then add the remaining sugar and the shoyu. Simmer until almost all of the juice has been absorbed. Transfer to a bowl and serve either hot or cold.

Note: This dish was created to cook slowly over a charcoal fire (hibachi) which traditional Japanese homes used to have burning throughout the day. It is still a popular dish, although nowadays it is usually cooked on a modern hob.

Spinach with Cockles in Mustard Sauce

Spinach with Cockles in Mustard Sauce

Karashi-ae

1 tablespoon sake (rice wine)
225 g (8 oz) cockles, cleaned
3 tablespoons shoyu (Japanese soy sauce), plus 1 teaspoon
1 teaspoon Japanese or other hot mustard
500 g (1 lb) spinach leaves, washed and trimmed
salt
1 teaspoon sesame seeds

Heat the sake in a small saucepan, add the cockles and heat through. Drain the cockles, reserving the juice.

Put 3 tablespoons shoyu and the mustard in a bowl and mix together. Add the cockles. Cook the spinach leaves in lightly salted boiling water for 30 seconds, then drain and plunge immediately into a bowl of ice-cold water. Drain again and squeeze out any excess water, then pour over the 1 teaspoon shoyu.

Add the cockle juice to the cockle mixture. Arrange the spinach in a serving bowl. Place the cockle mixture in the centre and garnish with sesame seeds.
Note: Cockles are available frozen. Thaw in their containers for approximately 2 hours in the refrigerator before reheating.

Vegetables with Tofu and Sesame Sauce

Shira-ae

6 abur-age (deep-fried bean curd)
½ fennel bulb
3 small carrots, peeled
250 ml (8 fl oz) Soup Stock (page 12)
1 block tofu (bean curd)
5 tablespoons white sesame seeds, toasted and crushed
2 tablespoons shiromiso (white soy bean paste)
3 tablespoons sugar
1 teaspoon salt

To garnish:
cucumber strips
carrot slice

Wash the abur-age in boiling water to remove the excess oil, then cut lengthways into 5 mm (¼ inch) slices. Cut the fennel and carrots into 5 cm (2 inch) strips.

Cook the abur-age, fennel and carrots in the stock for about 5 minutes until the carrots are tender but still crisp and most of the stock has evaporated. Leave to cool, then cut the vegetables into small pieces and place in a large serving bowl.

Wrap the tofu in a cloth and press down to squeeze out as much water as possible. Crush the tofu. Add the remaining ingredients, except the garnish, and mix well. Pour the tofu dressing over the vegetables and mix together, taking care not to crush the vegetables.

Garnish with cucumber strips and a carrot slice. Serve at room temperature, as a side dish.
Note: This is a most interesting tangy white dressing for cooked vegetables.

White Radish Salad

Sunomono Daikon

1 daikon (Japanese radish), about the size of a cucumber, peeled and finely grated
4 tablespoons vinegar
2 tablespoons sugar
pinch of salt
6 cm (2½ inch) piece cucumber, finely diced
1 persimmon, finely diced
1 teaspoon grated fresh horseradish
1 teaspoon grated fresh root ginger

Gently squeeze the daikon in a cloth to remove the excess liquid. Mix together the vinegar, sugar and salt and add to the daikon. Toss to coat. Add the remaining ingredients and mix well. Shape in small mounds and place on plates as an accompaniment.

31

Pressed Salad

Tsukemono

*15 cm (6 inch) piece daikon (Japanese radish),
peeled
2 medium carrots, peeled
225 g (8 oz) French beans, topped and tailed
salt*

*To serve:
Saubaizu sauce as for Vinegared Cucumber
(page 28)
1 tablespoon sesame seeds, toasted*

Cut the daikon and carrots into 5–7.5 cm (2–3 inch) lengths. Slice them into matchstick-size pieces. Cut the French beans into 5–7.5 cm (2–3 inch) pieces, depending on their length, then slice lengthways in half. Mix the vegetables together and place one-quarter in a large bowl. Sprinkle over about ½ teaspoon salt. Repeat with more vegetables and salt until all the shredded vegetables are placed in the bowl. Cover the vegetables with an upturned plate (a little smaller than the bowl), place a heavy weight on top and leave for at least 1 hour, preferably overnight.

When ready to eat the salad, remove the weight and pour off any excess water from the vegetables, pressing the plate firmly to extract as much liquid as possible. Remove the plate and mix the vegetables well, then add saubaizu sauce and mix well again. Transfer to individual salad bowls and sprinkle over the sesame seeds. Serve the pressed salad cold.

Note: Like rice and soup, Tsukemono is part of almost every Japanese meal. It is eaten with simple, everyday food, and is even served at the most formal of banquets. For a simple end to a meal serve this salad with a bowl of plain boiled rice.

Peach Flowers

Momo no Hana

*1 bunch large red radishes
1 tablespoon salt
100 ml (3½ fl oz) rice vinegar
2 tablespoons sugar
100 g (4 oz) mangetout, trimmed*

Wash the radishes and trim off the stems. Place a radish, trimmed side down, on a board between a pair of parallel hashi (chopsticks). Using a sharp knife and holding the radish steady with your other hand, finely slice the radish, making sure that the knife does not go all the way to the bottom (the hashi will help prevent this). Turn the radish 90° so that the incisions are parallel to the hashi. Again, finely slice the radish, creating a criss-cross effect. Repeat with the remaining radishes.

Place the radishes in a large bowl and sprinkle the salt all over them, mixing well. Put a small plate over the radishes, place heavy weights on top and leave pressed down overnight.

Drain off the water from the radishes, then mix together the vinegar and sugar and pour over the radishes. Cover again with the plate and weights and leave again overnight.

The following day, cook the mangetout in a saucepan of lightly salted boiling water for 2 to 3 minutes. Drain and rinse under cold running water to prevent further cooking.

Arrange the pickled radish 'flowers' on a plate and surround with the mangetout to resemble 'leaves'. Serve cold. *Serves 10*

Note: In Japan, turnips are used to make flowers, but Japanese turnips are closer to red radishes than they are to Western turnips, which is why red radishes are used here, with equally good effect. The 'flowers' should be prepared well in advance and the 'leaves' cooked on the day. Girls' Day in Japan is sometimes referred to as Peach Celebration, and these flowers are said to resemble peach blossom.

Sweet Black Mushrooms

Shiitake no Amani

*15 dried shiitake mushrooms, with large caps
450 ml (¾ pint) water
1½ teaspoons sugar
1–2 tablespoons mirin (sweet rice wine)
pinch of salt
2 teaspoons shoyu (Japanese soy sauce)
shredded spring onion and carrot slices, to garnish*

Soak the mushrooms in warm water for 25 minutes. Drain, reserving the soaking liquid, then discard the mushroom stems. Leave the caps whole or slice each one into 5 pieces.

Pour the mushroom liquid slowly into a pan, taking care to avoid including the sandy sediment at the bottom which should be discarded. Add the mushrooms and boil for 5 minutes. Add the remaining ingredients and cook for 5 minutes; if liked, sprinkle in a little more mirin.

Remove from the heat and leave to stand for 10 minutes. Arrange the mushrooms in an attractive pattern on a serving plate. Garnish with the spring onion and carrot slices, placed in the centre to resemble a flower head. Serve at room temperature, as an appetizer or side dish.

Note: Shiitake is the legendary Black Forest mushroom so favoured by the Japanese and Chinese for its health-giving vitamins.

Shiitake mushrooms are available in dehydrated form in speciality shops and markets and, although it is possible to buy fresh shiitake, it is the dehydrated form that should be used in this recipe. Chew the succulent pieces slowly to appreciate their excellent flavour.

Peach Flowers; Pressed Salad; Sweet Black Mushrooms

Seaweed with Fried Bean Curd

Hijiki to Abur-age

5 tablespoons dry hijiki (brown algae seaweed)
2 abur-age (deep-fried bean curd)
1 teaspoon vegetable oil
150 ml (¼ pint) Soup Stock (page 12)
1 tablespoon mirin (sweet rice wine)
2½ teaspoons sugar
2 tablespoons shoyu (Japanese soy sauce)

Pick out as much sediment as possible from the hijiki, then wash and soak in cold water for 1 hour. Drain, then rinse thoroughly under cold running water to remove the sand. Strain in a fine sieve.

Wash the abur-age in boiling water to remove excess oil, then cut lengthways into 5 mm (¼ inch) slices.

Heat a frying pan, add the oil, then the hijiki. Fry for about 2 minutes, then add the abur-age and stock. Simmer, uncovered, for 5 minutes.

Add the remaining ingredients, stir well and cook for 7 minutes or until all the liquid has evaporated. Serve hot in warmed individual serving dishes.

Note: Japan is surrounded by water, so it is hardly surprising that seaweeds have become one of the major foodstuffs to the Japanese. These seaweeds are high in protein, starch, sugar, fat, vitamins A, B_1, B_2, calcium, phosphorus, iron and trace elements.

Mustard-pickled Aubergine

Nasu no Karashi

*1 medium aubergine, or 6 small Japanese
elongated aubergines
750 ml (1¼ pints) water
1 tablespoon salt*

*Dressing:
1 teaspoon dry mustard
3 tablespoons shoyu (Japanese soy sauce)
3 tablespoons mirin (sweet rice wine)
3 tablespoons sugar*

Cut the aubergine crossways into slices about 3 mm (⅛ inch) thick, then cut the slices into quarters. Soak in the water, with the salt added, for 1 hour.

Meanwhile, make the dressing: put all the ingredients in a bowl and stir well.

Drain the aubergine and pat dry with kitchen paper towels. Arrange in a glass serving bowl and pour over the dressing.

Cover with plastic wrap and chill in the refrigerator for several hours or overnight before serving, to allow the flavours to develop.
Note: This spicy pickle will add zest to any dinner. It is an unusual way to blend ingredients.

Cabbage Pickles

Nappa no Tsukemono

*1 large head of napa (Chinese cabbage), quartered
3 tablespoons coarse salt
4 tablespoons seedless raisins or stoned prunes
250 ml (8 fl oz) water
3 dried chillies*

Put the napa in a glass bowl, sprinkling the layers with the salt. Add the remaining ingredients and mix well until the salt has dissolved.

Place a saucer on top of the cabbage, put a heavy weight on top, then leave to marinate for 12 hours.

Discard the raisins or prunes and wash the cabbage quickly. Squeeze out the excess moisture, then slice the cabbage into bite-sized pieces. Serve cold. *Serves 4 to 6*
Note: For extra flavour, add a little shoyu (Japanese soy sauce), monosodium glutamate and freshly grated root ginger mixed with a little sugar, before serving.

Pickles appear on every Japanese menu; they go especially well with the blandness of the rice and tea; and they also help to clear the palate of lingering tastes such as fish. Many methods of preserving vegetables are used, including brine, rice bran, soy bean paste and mustard.

This recipe, using brine, is one of the simplest ways of preserving. If kept in the brine in the refrigerator, the napa will keep for about 1 week.

Spinach with Bonito Flakes

Horenso no Ohitashi

*500 g (1 lb) fresh young spinach leaves
salt
2½ tablespoons shoyu (Japanese soy sauce)
4–5 tablespoons Soup Stock (page 12)
4 tablespoons katsuo-bushi (dried bonito flakes), to
garnish*

Trim the spinach, discarding any thick stalks. Blanch in a large saucepan of lightly salted boiling water for 2 minutes. Drain, plunge into a bowl of ice-cold water to prevent further cooking, then drain again thoroughly. Squeeze out the water from the spinach with your hands, then spread out on a board or large plate. Sprinkle ½ tablespoon of the shoyu over the spinach, then squeeze out more liquid.

Put the stock and remaining shoyu in a wide, shallow tin. Add the spinach and soak in the sauce for about 5 minutes, then return to the board, arranging all the leaves side by side. Gently squeeze the sauce out of the spinach into the tin and reserve. Cut the spinach into 4–5 cm (1½–2 inch) pieces and place in a bowl. Garnish with the dried bonito flakes and sprinkle over the reserved sauce. Serve cold.

Note: This is one of the simplest but most nutritious vegetable dishes as the high iron content of the spinach complements the protein in the bonito flakes.

Tree Oyster Mushrooms

Shimeji

225 g (8 oz) fresh shimeji (tree oyster mushrooms)
1½ teaspoons butter
1 garlic clove, peeled and crushed
1 teaspoon sake (rice wine)
3 tablespoons chicken stock
salt
freshly ground black pepper

Tear the shimeji into bite-sized pieces. Melt the butter in a frying pan over low heat. Add the garlic and stir-fry for 30 seconds, then add the shimeji and sake. Stir-fry for 1 minute, then add the remaining ingredients and cook for 2 minutes. Serve immediately, as a side dish.
Note: The shimeji has been cultivated in Japan for years as a fresh fungus 'vegetable'. It is now becoming more widely available because it can be grown easily under controlled conditions. In damp woods, one can find the wild species of shimeji, *Pleurotus ostreatus*. It has a slight shellfish flavour.

Chilli-flavoured Burdock

Kimpira

3 long gobo (burdock roots), skinned
1 small carrot, peeled
1 tablespoon vegetable oil
1 tablespoon shoyu (Japanese soy sauce)
1 tablespoon sugar
pinch of salt
pinch of dried chilli pepper flakes

Cut the gobo and carrot into paper-thin 1 cm (½ inch) wide strips, using a vegetable peeler. Place in a bowl of cold water until ready for use, then drain and pat dry with kitchen paper towels.

Heat a frying pan. When hot, add the oil, then the vegetables, and stir-fry for about 2 minutes until tender but still crisp.

Add the remaining ingredients and stir-fry for 2 minutes. Serve hot or at room temperature.
Note: This dish can be served as an appetizer or as an accompaniment to any meal. Burdock is considered a nuisance weed in the West, but in Japan gobo, the root, is used as a vegetable. It is an acquired taste, however, and you may have to try it several times before you like it. The chilli pepper gives the dish its name and zip.

From left to right: Tree Oyster Mushrooms; Cabbage Pickles; Mustard-Pickled Aubergine

35

Meat & Poultry

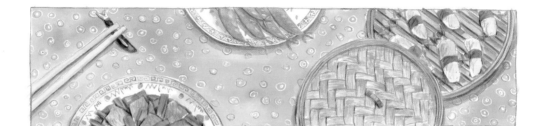

Prior to 1868 and the end of the 300-year-long Tonkugawa era, Japan was closed to foreign visitors. The exception was the trading port of Nagasaki, where foreigners were allowed to mix with the Japanese. These people, who were known as *nanban* (or barbarians), introduced the habit of eating meat. Today, meat is still a luxury, as the mountainous landscape does not lend itself to the rearing of large herds of cattle.

Beef and Radish Juice Fondue

Karibayaki

750 g (1½ lb) beef steak, cut into thin slices
5 spring onions, cut into 2.5 cm (1 inch) lengths
350 g (12 oz) bamboo shoots, halved and cut into very thin slices
225 g (8 oz) parsley sprigs
225 g (8 oz) aubergine, cut into very thin slices
500 g (1 lb) matsutake mushrooms, torn into bite-size pieces
750 g (1½ lb) daikon (Japanese radish)
1½ tablespoons shoyu (Japanese soy sauce)
crushed Japanese pepper
75 g (3 oz) beef suet

Sauce:
shoyu (Japanese soy sauce)
sake (rice wine)
mirin (sweet rice wine)
sugar

Arrange the steak, spring onions, bamboo shoots, parsley, aubergine and mushrooms on a serving plate.

Grate the radish and squeeze out the juice. Reserve 250 ml (8 fl oz) of the juice and mix with the shoyu and pepper to taste. Place this dip in a serving bowl.

Make the sauce using three parts shoyu, two parts sake, one part mirin and two parts sugar. Mix well until the sugar has dissolved, then pour into a bowl.

Heat the suet in an electric frying pan in the centre of the table. Take a piece of steak or vegetable, coat it in the shoyu sauce and place it in the frying pan. Cook until tender, then dip into the radish sauce and eat. *Serves 4 to 6*

Grilled Ginger Pork

Shoga-yaki

2 × 175–225 g (6–8 oz) pork fillets
5 cm (2 inch) piece fresh root ginger, peeled and grated
4 tablespoons shoyu (Japanese soy sauce)
grated daikon (Japanese radish), to garnish

Put the pork fillets in a shallow dish, add the grated ginger and shoyu. Leave to marinate in a cold place for at least 30 minutes.

Wrap each fillet in foil, seal the edges and reserve any marinade in the dish. Place under a preheated hot grill for 5 minutes, then turn the grill down to low and continue cooking for a further 20 to 25 minutes, or until the pork is thoroughly cooked.

Unwrap the pork and cut each fillet into 1 cm (½ inch) slices. Place on warmed individual plates. Pour the meat juices from the foil into a small saucepan and add any reserved marinade. If there is not enough sauce add a few spoonfuls of water and shoyu to taste. Bring to the boil and simmer for about 5 minutes, then pour over the meat. Serve hot.

Note: An easy, economical dish, which nonetheless is delicious enough to be served at dinner parties. Serve with French beans and plain boiled rice, if wished. Garnish with grated daikon.

Grilled Ginger Pork; Vinegared Cucumber (page 28); Grilled Skewered Chicken (page 44)

Pork with Shredded White Cabbage

Tonkatsu

750 g (1½ lb) pork fillet
salt
freshly ground black pepper
plain flour for coating
2 eggs, lightly beaten
about 100 g (4 oz) dried breadcrumbs
10 cm (4 inch) wedge hard white cabbage
vegetable oil for deep-frying

Tonkatsu sauce:
shoyu (Japanese soy sauce)
sake (rice wine)
Worcestershire sauce
Japanese mustard

Cut the pork fillet crossways into 1 cm (½ inch) slices.

Sprinkle lightly with salt and pepper, then dust with flour, shaking off any excess. Dip each piece of pork into the beaten eggs, then coat in the breadcrumbs. Press lightly so that the breadcrumbs adhere to the meat.

Separate the cabbage leaves, then cut each one in half, discarding the thick and tough central stalks. Pile the leaves on top of each other, then cut into fine shreds. Arrange one-quarter of the shredded cabbage on each of 4 individual plates so that half of the plate is covered.

To make the tonkatsu sauce: combine all the ingredients in a bowl or jug, adjusting the quantities to taste. Pour into 4 individual bowls.

Heat the oil in a deep-fat frier or deep frying pan to 180°C/350°F. Gently slide in the pork pieces one at a time. Deep-fry in batches for 3 to 5 minutes until golden brown, then remove with a perforated spoon and drain on a wire rack. When all the pork has been cooked, arrange the slices on the plates with the cabbage. Serve immediately, with the tonkatsu sauce for dipping.

Note: This deep-fried, breaded pork is a popular family supper or lunch dish in Japan. It is simple, economical and filling, yet also extremely delicious.

Beef with Vegetables

Sukiyaki

500 g (1 lb) sirloin or topside of beef
4 heads of Chinese leaves
1 bunch watercress
2 thin leeks, white part only
8 button mushrooms
100 g (4 oz) firm tofu (bean curd)
200 g (7 oz) shirataki (yam noodles), or
fine vermicelli
1 small piece of beef fat (suet)

To serve:
Soup Stock (page 12)
shoyu (Japanese soy sauce)
mirin (sweet rice wine)
sake (rice wine)
sugar
4 eggs

Freeze the meat for 45 minutes, leave for 10 minutes on a board, then cut into wafer-thin slices with a very sharp knife. Arrange the meat on a platter. Cover and chill in the refrigerator.

Wash the Chinese leaves, cut in half lengthways, then cut into 5 cm (2 inch) lengths. Wash and trim the watercress. Slice the leeks diagonally. Wipe and trim the mushrooms. Cut the tofu into 4 cm (1½ inch) cubes. Cook the shirataki (if using) in boiling water for 3 minutes, then drain. If using vermicelli, soak it in boiling water for 10 minutes, then drain. Arrange the vegetables, tofu and noodles on a platter.

Place a cast-iron frying pan on a portable cooking stove in the centre of the dining table. Surround with the platters of raw ingredients and with jugs of stock, shoyu, mirin and sake, and a pot of sugar.

Melt a little beef fat in the pan, then add a few slices of meat and cook until lightly browned. Add a selection of the other raw ingredients, then pour in stock, soy sauce, mirin, sake and sugar to taste. Each diner beats an egg lightly in his or her bowl, takes a selection of the cooked ingredients and mixes them with the egg.

Note: Most Japanese families have special sukiyaki pans to cook this popular dish at the table, but a heavy-based frying pan and a portable cooking stove will do the job just as well. Sukiyaki is very informal – the host or hostess cooks the first amount of meat and vegetables at the table, adding flavouring ingredients to his or her taste. After the first cooking it is every man for himself, and ingredients are selected, cooked and flavoured according to individual tastes. Bowls of plain boiled rice are served to each guest to be eaten alongside the sukiyaki.

38

Japanese 'Roast' Beef

Wafu Roast Beef

750 g (1½ lb) sirloin of beef
1 garlic clove, peeled and sliced
100 ml (3½ fl oz) shoyu (Japanese soy sauce)
100 ml (3½ fl oz) sake (rice wine)
1½ teaspoons sugar

To serve:
2 spring onions, trimmed and finely chopped
2.5 cm (1 inch) fresh root ginger, peeled and grated
parsley sprigs, to garnish

Put the beef in a deep saucepan with the garlic, shoyu, sake and sugar. Put an otoshi-buta (small wooden lid) or small upturned plate on top of the joint, cover the pan with a lid, place over high heat and bring to the boil. Lower the heat and simmer for 10 minutes, shaking the saucepan occasionally so that the meat does not stick.

Transfer the meat to a board, cut in half and check the extent of the cooking. If the meat is too rare for your liking, return it to the saucepan and cook for a further few minutes. When the meat is cooked, remove the saucepan from the heat. Leave the meat to cool in the liquid, covered with the lid.

Slice the meat thinly, then arrange on individual plates and garnish with parsley sprigs. Serve cold, with the cooking liquid from the meat served in individual bowls, and the prepared spring onions and ginger (see note).

Note: Wafu Roast Beef is traditionally served with finely chopped spring onions and grated fresh root ginger. Each person mixes a little spring onion and ginger with some of the sauce, then dips a slice of meat into it before eating. If you prefer, mustard can be substituted for the ginger and spring onion. Japanese mustard, which is very hot, is available from Japanese supermarkets and other oriental stores.

Simmered Pork with Soy Sauce

Kakuni

500 g (1 lb) boneless leg or loin of pork
200 ml (7 fl oz) sake (rice wine)
about 400 ml (14 fl oz) Soup Stock (page 12) or water
2 tablespoons mirin (sweet rice wine)
2 tablespoons sugar
7 tablespoons shoyu (Japanese soy sauce)
100 ml (3½ fl oz) katsuo-bushi (dried bonito flakes)

Put the pork in a saucepan and pour over the sake. Leave to marinate for 30 minutes, turning the pork over from time to time so that it absorbs the sake evenly.

Pour enough stock or water into the pan to cover the pork. Place over high heat and bring to the boil, then skim with a perforated spoon. Lower the heat, cover the pan and simmer for about 1 hour.

Lift out the pork, reserving 450–600 ml (¾–1 pint) cooking liquid. Cut the pork into 4 equal pieces, then place in a clean saucepan with the reserved cooking liquid. Add the mirin and sugar and bring to the boil, then lower the heat, cover and simmer for 30 minutes. Add 4 tablespoons of the shoyu and the katsuo-bushi, cover again and simmer for a further 2 hours, adding the remaining shoyu after 1 hour. Transfer the meat to a warmed serving dish and serve hot.

Note: This dish originated in the port of Nagasaki. Unlike the rest of Japan, this port has been open to foreign visitors for many centuries, and it was due to the influence of Chinese and Western traders that the first meat dishes came from this area (the Japanese Buddhist law forbids the eating of meat). In Japan, belly pork is normally used for Kakuni, but this may be too fatty for most Western tastes. Leg or loin of pork is leaner, and it will be beautifully soft and tender at the end of the long cooking time.

Japanese 'Roast' Beef; Beef with Vegetables

Beef and Vegetables Cooked in Broth

Shabu Shabu

750 g (1½ lb) sirloin or topside of beef
4 heads of Chinese leaves
2 thin leeks, white part only
1 bunch watercress
8 medium button mushrooms
100 g (4 oz) firm tofu (bean curd)
150 g (5 oz) canned bamboo shoots, drained
10 cm (4 inch) square konbu (dried kelp)
2 spring onions, finely chopped
1 small daikon (Japanese radish), peeled and grated, or momiji-oroshi (Plain Fried Place, page 48)
4 lemon wedges
150 ml (¼ pint) shoyu (Japanese soy sauce)

Sesame sauce:
3 tablespoons sesame paste (tahini)
100 ml (3½ fl oz) Soup Stock (page 12)
2 tablespoons shoyu (Japanese soy sauce)
1 tablespoon mirin (sweet rice wine)
1½ teaspoons sugar
1 tablespoon sake (rice wine)
1 teaspoon chilli sauce (optional)

Prepare the meat, Chinese leaves, leeks, watercress, mushrooms and tofu as for Beef with Vegetables (page 38). Cook the bamboo shoots in boiling water for 3 minutes, drain, then cut into half-moon shapes about 5 mm (¼ inch) thick, if not already sliced. Arrange the meat, tofu and vegetables on a large serving platter.

To make the sesame sauce: put the sesame paste in a serving bowl and add the stock, shoyu, mirin, sugar and sake. Mix well and add the chilli sauce, if liked.

Put the konbu in a donabe (earthenware pot) or flameproof casserole and fill two-thirds full with cold water. Bring to the boil and immediately remove the konbu. Transfer the pot or casserole to a portable cooking stove in the centre of the dining table and bring the water to the boil again.

Put the platter of meat, tofu and vegetables on the table, with the bowl of sesame sauce and separate bowls of chopped spring onions, grated daikon or momiji-oroshi and lemon wedges. Pour the shoyu into a small jug. Set the table so that each guest has 2 sauce bowls, one for the sesame sauce and the other for a sauce which guests make themselves by mixing together spring onions, daikon or momiji-oroshi, a squeeze of lemon juice and shoyu to taste. Guests then help themselves to ingredients, cook them in the broth and dip them in the sauce of their choice before eating.
Note: The ingredients for Shabu Shabu are basically the same as for Beef with Vegetables (page 38), but they are cooked in a broth. The name Shabu Shabu is an onomatopoeia describing the sound of washing. Wafer-thin slices of beef are picked up with hashi (chopsticks), dipped into broth and swished from side to side as if washing clothes in water.

Pork on Skewers

Buta Teriyaki

1 kg (2–2¼ lb) pork fillet, thinly sliced
1 teaspoon grated fresh root ginger
1 medium onion, peeled and finely chopped
5 tablespoons shoyu (Japanese soy sauce)
4 tablespoons sugar
4 tablespoons sake (rice wine)

Put all the ingredients in a bowl, mix well, then leave to marinate for at least 1 hour.

Thread the pork on to 4 skewers, reserving the marinade. Grill for 3 minutes on each side, basting frequently with the marinade. Serve immediately.
Note: Pork marinated in teriyaki sauce has an exquisite flavour, especially if cooked over a charcoal grill. If this is not available, an ordinary grill may be used, although the flavour will not be quite so good.

If liked, spring onions, mushroom caps and strips of green pepper can be added to the skewers, alternating with the pork. Use bamboo skewers if possible. As a variation, chicken, beef, prawns or fish may be used instead of pork.

40

Mixed Grill

Mixed Grill

Teppanyaki

*4 sirloin or fillet steaks, or 4 boned chicken
breasts, cut into chunks
8 cooked, unpeeled prawns
2 medium courgettes, sliced into julienne strips
2 medium onions, peeled and finely sliced
225 g (8 oz) fresh bean sprouts
225 g (8 oz) button mushrooms
1 tablespoon vegetable oil*

Ponzu (tart sauce):
*120 ml (4 fl oz) shoyu (Japanese soy sauce)
120 ml (4 fl oz) lime or lemon juice
4 tablespoons mirin (sweet rice wine)*

Karashi jyoyu (mustard sauce):
*2 teaspoons dry mustard
2 teaspoons hot water
3 tablespoons shoyu (Japanese soy sauce)
2 tablespoons rice vinegar
1 teaspoon sesame seed oil*

Arrange the beef or chicken, prawns and vegetables artistically on a large serving plate.

To make the ponzu sauce: mix together all the ingredients and pour into individual dishes. To make the karashi jyoyu sauce: mix the mustard and water to a paste, then add the remaining ingredients. Pour into individual dishes.

Heat a griddle or electric frying pan at the table. Add the oil, then some of the meat and prawns. As the meat becomes tender, add a few vegetables to the pan and cook until they are tender but still crisp.

Serve the meat, prawns and vegetables as they are ready, letting the guests dip them into their sauces while more teppanyaki is cooking.

Note: *Teppan* means 'iron', and *yaki* means 'to fry'. Any combination of meat, seafood or poultry can be used with vegetables in season for this dish. As illustrated, vegetables, such as radishes, chopped fresh spinach leaves, sliced green or red peppers, mangetout, French beans and spring onions are all suitable. Traditionally, a heavy iron griddle is used at the table, but an electric frying pan may be used instead.

At Japanese speciality restaurants, talented cooks bow before the diners and act out a 'show', waving sharp knives in the air while they prepare this scrumptious meal before your very eyes.

Raw Beef

Yukhwe

225 g (8 oz) sirloin steak
1 garlic clove, peeled and crushed
2 teaspoons sesame seed oil
½ teaspoon sesame seeds
1½ teaspoons sugar
½ teaspoon salt
½ teaspoon freshly ground white pepper
1 firm pear
½ cucumber
4 quail's or hen's egg yolks

Freeze the meat for 45 minutes; leave for 10 minutes on a board, then shred with a very sharp knife. Leave the shredded meat in the refrigerator until thoroughly defrosted.

Mix the meat with the crushed garlic, sesame seed oil, sesame seeds, sugar, salt and pepper.

Peel and core the pear, then shred finely. Peel the cucumber, then cut in half lengthways and scoop out the seeds with a sharp-edged teaspoon. Finely shred the flesh. Divide the pear and cucumber shreds equally between 4 individual plates.

Spoon one-quarter of the meat mixture on each bed of pear and cucumber. Top each serving with an egg yolk and serve immediately.

Note: Yukhwe is served as a starter. The yolk of a raw egg is mixed with the meat before eating.

42

Meat with Miso

Niku no Miso-yaki

750 g (1½ lb) beef flank steak, in one piece
2 tablespoons vegetable oil
toasted sesame seeds, to garnish

Marinade:
4 tablespoons akamiso (red soy bean paste)
2 tablespoons shoyu (Japanese soy sauce)
1½ tablespoons sugar
1 teaspoon grated fresh root ginger
1 spring onion, chopped

Cut the meat lengthways through the middle, then cut into thin slices across the grain. Place the slices in a bowl with the akamiso, shoyu, sugar, ginger and spring onion. Mix well, then leave to marinate for 10 minutes.

Place a frying pan over high heat. Add the oil, then the meat and marinade. Stir-fry for about 2 minutes. Serve hot, sprinkled with toasted sesame seeds.

Note: Akamiso (Japanese red soy bean paste) gives meat an entirely different flavour. Served with hot steamed rice and salad, this dish makes a quick family meal.

Chicken Cooked with Vegetables

Iridori

2 dried shiitake mushrooms
100 g (4 oz) canned gobo (burdock root), drained, or fresh parsnip
100 g (4 oz) canned bamboo shoots, drained
75 g (3 oz) canned renkon (lotus root) or water chestnuts, drained
1 medium carrot, peeled
½ cake kon-nyaku (arum root)
5 tablespoons vegetable oil
6½ tablespoons shoyu (Japanese soy sauce)
1 chicken leg, boned
1 teaspoon finely chopped fresh root ginger
a little sake (rice wine)
4 tablespoons sugar
Soup Stock (page 12) or water
2 tablespoons mirin (sweet rice wine)

Soak the mushrooms in warm water for 20 to 25 minutes. Drain them, discard the stalks, and cut the caps into bite-sized pieces. Cut the remaining vegetables into bite-sized pieces. The carrot can be cut decoratively into small flower shapes, if liked. Break the kon-nyaku into bite-sized pieces. Heat 1 tablespoon of the oil in a heavy-based frying pan, add the kon-nyaku pieces and fry for 1 to 2 minutes, sprinkling on ½ tablespoon of the shoyu. Remove from the pan and set aside.

Chop the chicken meat into slightly larger pieces than the vegetables. Heat another tablespoon of the oil in the frying pan. Add the chicken pieces and chopped ginger. Sprinkle with a little sake, half of the sugar and 3 tablespoons of the remaining shoyu. Stir-fry for about 2 minutes, or until lightly browned. Remove the chicken from the pan with a perforated spoon and set aside. Reserve the pan juices.

Heat the remaining oil in a shallow saucepan. Add the mushrooms, vegetables and the kon-nyaku and fry for 1 minute. Add the reserved pan juices from the chicken and enough stock or water to just cover the vegetables. Put an otoshi-buta (small wooden lid) or small upturned plate inside the pan so that the vegetables are held down tightly. Cover the pan with a lid and simmer for 5 to 8 minutes, until the vegetables are lightly cooked.

Add the remaining sugar, replace the otoshi-buta or plate and the pan lid and cook for a further 10 minutes. Add the mirin and the remaining shoyu, cover and continue cooking until the juice has been absorbed. Add the chicken pieces, cook over high heat for 30 seconds, then leave until cold before serving.

Note: Iridori looks most attractive in its serving bowl, when garnished with boiled carrot 'flowers' and cooked fresh garden peas. Ginnan or gingko nuts could also be used as a garnish.

Meat with Miso; Plain Steamed Rice (page 18); Vinegared Cucumber (page 28)

Chicken Teriyaki

Tori no Teriyaki

4 chicken legs
3 tablespoons vegetable oil
1 tablespoon mirin (sweet rice wine)
1 tablespoon sugar
watercress sprigs, to garnish
sansho powder, to serve

Marinade:
3 tablespoons shoyu (Japanese soy sauce)
1 tablespoon sake (rice wine)
1 tablespoon mirin (sweet rice wine)
1 teaspoon ginger juice (see note)

Bone the chicken legs, then spike the skin with a fork to prevent the skin shrinking during cooking. Put the chicken in a shallow dish. Prepare the marinade by mixing together the shoyu, sake, mirin and ginger juice in a jug, then pour over the chicken and leave to marinate for 20 to 30 minutes.

Heat the oil in a heavy-based frying pan. Remove the chicken from the marinade, place skin side down in the pan and fry until the skin is lightly browned. Turn the chicken over and continue frying for about 10 minutes, until the chicken is tender when pierced with hashi (chopsticks).

Remove the chicken from the pan and pour off any excess oil. Add the marinade to the pan, then the mirin and sugar. Simmer for 2 to 3 minutes, then return the chicken legs to the pan and turn them over so that they are completely soaked in the pan juices.

Transfer the chicken to a board and slice thinly. Arrange the slices on a warmed serving platter and garnish with watercress. Serve hot, with sansho powder.

Note: In Japan, hashi (chopsticks) are used both as cooking utensils and for eating. For this recipe they are used to test if the chicken meat is tender.

Ginger juice is obtained by grating fresh root ginger, then squeezing out the juice.

Grilled Skewered Chicken

Yakitori

2 chicken legs
2 thin leeks, white part only, or 2 large spring onions

Tare sauce:
65 ml (2½ fl oz) shoyu (Japanese soy sauce)
65 ml (2½ fl oz) mirin (sweet rice wine)
2 tablespoons sugar
2 teaspoons plain flour

Bone the chicken legs, then cut the meat into 24 bite-sized pieces. Cut the leeks or spring onions into 16 pieces. Put all the ingredients for the tare sauce in a small saucepan. Bring to the boil, stirring, then simmer for 10 minutes, or until the sauce reduces to about two-thirds of its original volume. Remove from the heat.

Thread 3 pieces of chicken and 2 pieces of leek or spring onion alternately on to 8 Japanese bamboo skewers. Grill over a charcoal barbecue or under a conventional grill until browned, then remove from the heat and spoon on the tare sauce. Return to the heat for a few more minutes, then remove and coat with more sauce. Repeat this process a few times until all of the tare sauce is used and the chicken is cooked.

Peanut Chicken

Tori Amazu-peanut

1 egg
2 tablespoons cornflour
½ teaspoon salt
6 chicken breasts, skinned and boned
vegetable oil for deep-frying
50 g (2 oz) peanuts, chopped
1 spring onion, chopped

Sauce:
4 tablespoons rice vinegar
120 ml (4 fl oz) water
4 tablespoons sugar
120 ml (4 fl oz) tomato ketchup
2 tablespoons cornflour
½ teaspoon salt

Lightly beat the egg with the cornflour and salt to make a batter. Coat the chicken breasts with the batter. Heat the oil in a deep frying pan and fry the chicken breasts until golden brown and cooked through.

Meanwhile make the sauce. Place all the ingredients in a saucepan and bring to the boil, stirring. Simmer until thickened.

Drain the chicken on kitchen paper towels and slice. Arrange on a serving dish and pour over the sauce. Sprinkle with the peanuts and spring onion. *Serves 6*

44

Chicken-stuffed Cucumbers

Kyuri Toriniku-zume

15 small cucumbers, each about 15 cm (6 inches) long
vegetable oil for frying
225 g (8 oz) chicken, minced
1 tablespoon finely chopped spring onion
1½ tablespoons white sesame seeds, toasted
1 small red pepper, cored, seeded and minced
1½ teaspoons shoyu (Japanese soy sauce)
1 teaspoon sugar
1½ teaspoons salt
600 ml (1 pint) Soup Stock (page 12)
1 tablespoon cornflour
1 tablespoon water

Trim the ends off the cucumbers, then make six lengthways slits around each one. Heat a little oil in a frying pan, add the cucumbers, in batches, and fry until golden but not brown. Drain on kitchen paper towels.

Mix together the chicken, spring onion, sesame seeds, red pepper, shoyu, sugar and ½ teaspoon of the salt. Press this mixture into the slits in the cucumbers until the cucumbers bulge. Make sure the stuffing will not fall out during cooking.

Place the stock and remaining salt in a saucepan and bring to the boil. Add the cucumbers and simmer gently for 20 to 30 minutes or until the chicken stuffing is cooked. Drain the cucumbers, reserving the cooking liquid, and place in serving dishes. Blend the cornflour with the water and add to the cooking liquid. Simmer, stirring, until thickened. Pour the sauce over the cucumbers before serving. *Serves 5*

Chicken and Vegetable Rice

Gomoku Itame Gohan

575 g (1¼ lb) Steamed Rice (page 18)
4 tablespoons seasoned rice vinegar
1 tablespoon vegetable oil
2 chicken breasts, skinned, boned and thinly sliced
1 carrot, thinly sliced diagonally
12 French beans, thinly sliced diagonally
5 mushrooms, sliced
1 teaspoon sugar
3 tablespoons shoyu (Japanese soy sauce)

Allow the rice to cool, then mix in the vinegar.

Heat the oil in a frying pan. Add the chicken and stir-fry until lightly browned. Add the carrot and beans and cook, stirring frequently, for about 10 minutes or until just tender. Stir in the mushrooms and cook for 2 minutes more. Add the sugar and shoyu, and mix well. Remove from heat and leave to cool, then mix in rice.

Chicken Cooked with Vegetables (page 42); Grilled Skewered Chicken

Chicken with Prawns and Vegetables

Umani

4 dried shiitake mushrooms
4 uncooked Dublin Bay prawns
salt
175 ml (6 fl oz) Soup Stock (page 12)
3 tablespoons shoyu (Japanese soy sauce)
3 tablespoons sugar
24 mangetout
225 g (8 oz) boned chicken breast, diced
4 tablespoons sake (rice wine)
450 g (1 lb) fresh bamboo shoots

Soak the mushrooms in warm water for 25 minutes.

Drop the prawns into boiling salted water and simmer until pink. Drain well, then peel and devein. Place the stock, shoyu, sugar and 1 teaspoon salt in the saucepan and bring to the boil. Add the prawns and simmer for 2 minutes. Drain, reserving the liquid.

Drop the mangetout into boiling salted water and simmer for 1 minute. Drain and add to the prawn liquid. Simmer for 1 minute longer. Drain, reserving the liquid.

Add the chicken and sake to the prawn liquid and sim-mer until the chicken is tender. Drain, reserving the liquid.

Drain the mushrooms, discard the stalks, and slice the caps. Add the bamboo shoots to the liquid and simmer until almost tender. Add the mushrooms and simmer with the bamboo shoots until both vegetables are tender. Return all the other ingredients to the pan and heat through.

Marinated Chicken Legs

Tori no Komi-yaki

4 tablespoons shoyu (Japanese soy sauce)
6 tablespoons mirin (sweet rice wine)
1 tablespoon white sesame seeds, toasted
1 small red pepper, cored, seeded and minced
1 spring onion, minced
5 chicken legs
vegetable oil for frying

Mix together the shoyu, mirin, sesame seeds, red pepper and spring onion in a shallow dish. Add the chicken legs and turn to coat. Leave to marinate for at least 2 hours, turning occasionally.

Lightly oil a frying pan and heat. Add the chicken legs and fry for about 15 minutes or until cooked through and golden brown on all sides. Turn and baste with the marinade from time to time. *Serves 5*

Chicken Deep-fried with Seaweed; Chicken with Prawns and Vegetables

Chicken Deep-fried with Seaweed

Chicken Oharame

175 g (6 oz) boned chicken breast, skinned
1 tablespoon shoyu (Japanese soy sauce)
1 tablespoon sake (rice wine)
½ sheet of nori (dried lava paper), cut into 1 cm (½ inch) wide strips
½ egg white, lightly beaten
vegetable oil for deep-frying

Cut the chicken into strips, about 5 cm × 5 mm (2 × ¼ inch). Mix the chicken strips with the shoyu and sake and leave to marinate for 1 hour.

Take four or five chicken strips in one hand. With the other hand, dip one end of a seaweed strip into the egg white and wrap around the centre of the chicken strips. Deep-fry in hot oil until the chicken is cooked through and tender. Drain on kitchen paper towels.

Chicken in Broth

Mizutaki

8 dried shiitake mushrooms
1 × 1.25 kg (2½–2¾ lb) chicken, boned and cut into 2.5 cm (1 inch) chunks
1 green pepper, cored, seeded and cut into long strips
½ cucumber, cut into strips
few carrots, peeled and trimmed
few mangetout, trimmed
1 block tofu (bean curd), cut into 2.5 cm (1 inch) cubes (optional)
1 medium napa (Chinese cabbage), sliced into 2.5 cm (1 inch) strips
few spring onions, cut into 5 cm (2 inch) lengths
1 litre (1¾ pints) Soup Stock (page 12)
1 tablespoon sake (rice wine)
1 small piece of konbu (dried kelp) (optional)

Gomatare (sesame sauce):
1 tablespoon shiromiso (white soy bean paste)
4 tablespoons sesame seeds, toasted and crushed
3 tablespoons mirin (sweet rice wine)
1 tablespoon sugar
2½ tablespoons shoyu (Japanese soy sauce)
120 ml (4 fl oz) Soup Stock (page 12)
½ teaspoon salad oil

Soak the mushrooms in warm water for 25 minutes. Drain the mushrooms, squeeze them dry, then discard the stems and slice the caps into thin strips.

Arrange the chicken and vegetables artistically on a large serving plate. Mix together all the sauce ingredients and divide between individual serving bowls.

Put the stock in a pan and stand in the centre of the table. Bring the stock to the boil, add the sake, konbu, if using, and the chicken and cook for 15 minutes. Let guests help themselves to chicken and vegetables, cooking the vegetables in the bubbling broth as required. Serve the sauce as a dip.

Note: Literally translated, *mizutaki* means 'water cooking'. This dish is traditionally cooked in a pan shaped like an angel cake pan with a chimney in the centre where hot charcoals are buried to provide the heat supply for the cooking. An electric frying pan or fondue dish can be used instead, so that guests can cook their own chicken and vegetables at the table.

Appearance plays a very important part in the art of Japanese cooking. Try to arrange the vegetables as artistically as possible on the serving dish – they should look like a beautiful picture.

Chicken Rice

Toriniku Donburi

3½ tablespoons shoyu (Japanese soy sauce)
2 tablespoons mirin (sweet rice wine)
175 g (6 oz) boned cooked chicken breast, sliced
1 litre (1¾ pints) chicken stock (made with the chicken carcass and giblets)
500 g (1 lb) Japanese medium-grain rice

Mix together the shoyu and mirin in a small dish. Add the chicken and turn to coat. Leave to marinate for 15 to 20 minutes. Drain the chicken, reserving the marinade. Set the chicken aside.

Add the marinade to the stock and bring to the boil in a large saucepan. Add the rice, cover and cook gently for about 20 minutes or until the rice is tender and has absorbed all the liquid. Divide the rice between individual bowls and place the marinated chicken on top.

Braised Marinated Duck

Kamo no Tsukeyaki

1 × 2.5–2.75 kg (5–6 lb) duck, jointed
120 ml (4 fl oz) shoyu (Japanese soy sauce)
450 ml (¾ pint) sake (rice wine)
1 teaspoon grated fresh root ginger
salt
pepper
2 tablespoons vegetable oil
1 large onion, sliced
225 g (8 oz) mushrooms, sliced

Remove as much fat from the duck as possible. Mix together the shoyu, sake, ginger, and salt and pepper to taste in a shallow dish. Add the duck pieces and turn to coat. Leave to marinate for 4 hours or overnight, turning occasionally.

Drain the duck, reserving the marinade. Heat the oil in a flameproof casserole. Add the duck and brown on all sides. Add the onion and mushrooms and cook for a further 5 minutes. Pour off the fat from the pan and add the reserved marinade. Bring to the boil, then cover and simmer gently for 1½ hours or until the duck is very tender.

Fish & Shellfish

Japan is an island surrounded by rich fishing waters, and as only a small portion of the country is suitable for farming, the Japanese have to rely on the sea as a major source of food.
Many of the fish eaten in Japan are not available in the West, but alternative salt or freshwater fish, round or flat fish can be substituted.
The Japanese are well-known for their love of raw fish, and Sashimi is therefore one of the most famous national dishes. For Sashimi, only the freshest fish can be used, and great care is taken over its preparation and presentation.

Plain Fried Plaice

Karei no Kara-age

4 small plaice, scaled and gutted
salt
2–3 teaspoons sake (rice wine)
plain flour for coating
vegetable oil for deep-frying

To garnish:
momiji-oroshi (see note)
4 lemon wedges

Wash the fish and remove the heads. Cut 2 crosses in the skin on each side of the fish, then place on a wire rack. Sprinkle with salt and sake and leave for 10 minutes.

Coat the fish thoroughly in flour. Heat the oil in a deep frying pan to about 160°C/325°F. Deep-fry the plaice until the slits in the skin open up, then increase the heat to crisp up the fish. Remove and drain. To serve, garnish with momiji-oroshi and lemon wedges.
Note: To make momiji-oroshi (grated 'autumn leaves'), pierce a hole lengthways in a daikon with a hashi (chopstick). Insert red chillies into the daikon so that, when grated, the daikon is reddish in colour, like autumn leaves.

Cod's Roe Flower

Hana Tarako

225 g (8 oz) fresh cod's roe
salt
200 ml (7 fl oz) Soup Stock (page 12)
100 ml (3½ fl oz) sake (rice wine)
50 ml (2 fl oz) mirin (sweet rice wine)
3 tablespoons sugar
1 tablespoon shoyu (Japanese soy sauce)
100 g (4 oz) mangetout, lightly cooked

Wash the cod's roe in lightly salted water. Make a slit in the skin. Mix the stock in a saucepan with the sake, mirin, sugar, shoyu and ⅔ teaspoon salt. Bring to the boil, add the roe and cook for a few minutes. Lower the heat and simmer for about 20 minutes. Leave to cool.

Drain the cod's roe, discarding the cooking liquid, and cut into flower shapes, 2.5 cm (1 inch) thick. Divide the cod's roe 'flowers' and mangetout equally between 4 individual plates, sprinkling the mangetout lightly with salt. Serve cold.
Note: Crisp mangetout peas form the 'leaves' of these delicate and soft cod's roe 'flowers'.

Cod's Roe Flower; Plain Fried Plaice

Braised Fish

Nizakana

1 tablespoon vegetable oil
1 kg (2–2¼ lb) fresh salmon, cut into serving pieces
1 medium onion, peeled, halved and cut into 1 cm (½ inch) thick slices
1½ tablespoons sake (rice wine)
2 tablespoons water
4 tablespoons shoyu (Japanese soy sauce)
2½ tablespoons sugar
1 teaspoon freshly grated root ginger

Place a frying pan over moderate heat, add the oil, then the fish and onion. Mix the remaining ingredients together, then pour into the pan. Cover and simmer for about 10 minutes until the fish flakes easily when tested with a fork. Serve hot. *Serves 4 to 6*
Note: This dish makes a quick, simple meal with plenty of flavour. Serve with rice and a green vegetable, with shichimi and sansho as condiments, if liked.

Mackerel Sashimi

Saba no Sashimi

1 large fresh mackerel
2 tablespoons rice vinegar
5 cm (2 inch) piece fresh root ginger, peeled and grated
shoyu (Japanese soy sauce)

Gut the mackerel and remove the head, then wash the fish thoroughly and carefully fillet it. Pat dry with paper towels, but do not wash again or the fish will lose its texture.

Using fingers and working from the tail end, remove the transparent skin, leaving the silver pattern intact. Using tweezers, remove all the bones which are hidden in the centre of the mackerel fillets. Cut diagonally into slices about 2.5 cm (1 inch) thick.

Arrange the mackerel slices on a serving platter and sprinkle with the rice vinegar. Serve the grated ginger and shoyu separately.
Note: This dish is simple to make and serve; each person should mix ginger and shoyu to taste in a small bowl, then dip a piece of mackerel into it before eating.

Salmon with Sake Lees

Shake no Kasuzuke

4 fresh salmon steaks
1½ tablespoons salt

Marinade:
450 ml (¾ pint) kasu (rice wine lees)
225 g (8 oz) sugar

To serve:
1 small lettuce, shredded
½ small daikon (Japanese radish), puréed

Preparation for this dish should begin 11 days before serving. Put the salmon in a bowl and sprinkle both sides with the salt. Cover with plastic wrap or foil and leave in the refrigerator for 4 days to allow the flesh of the salmon to become firm.

Drain the fish well, then pat dry with kitchen paper towels. Mix together the marinade ingredients and use to coat both sides of the salmon. Place in a dish, cover, and keep in the refrigerator for 7 days before serving.

Remove most of the marinade from the salmon, then grill for about 7 minutes on one side only until the fish flakes easily when tested with a fork. Take care not to overcook as the marinade causes the fish to char easily.

Serve hot, with small mounds of shredded lettuce and puréed daikon.

Note: When fresh salmon is plentiful, this is an excellent way to preserve some for later use. This dish makes a quick entrée and will keep for several months in the refrigerator. The flavour of kasu goes well with salmon, but it is strongly flavoured and should therefore be eaten in small quantities — until you acquire a taste for it, that is!

Salt Grilled Fish

Sakana no Shioyaki

1 × 750 g (1½ lb) mackerel or red snapper
salt

To serve:
few lemon wedges
shoyu (Japanese soy sauce) (optional)

Remove the scales from the fish, leaving the skin intact. Clean the fish thoroughly and remove the head, if wished, then sprinkle lightly inside and out with salt. Leave to stand for about 30 minutes.

Make 3 diagonal slashes on the surface of the fish. Grill under a preheated grill for about 5 minutes on each side, until the fish flakes easily when tested with a fork; do not overcook.

Serve hot with lemon wedges. Hand shoyu separately, if liked.

Note: This method of preparing protein-rich fish is surprisingly simple — the fat in the skin of the fish oozes out during cooking and the salt creates moisture so that the flesh is deliciously moist. Hot steamed rice and green tea make good accompaniments.

Marinated Mackerel

Tatsuta-age

2 medium mackerel, total weight about 750 g
(1½ lb), filleted
4 tablespoons shoyu (Japanese soy sauce)
2 tablespoons sake (rice wine)
1 teaspoon ginger juice (see note)
50 g (2 oz) cornflour
vegetable oil for deep-frying
8 small button mushrooms, wiped and trimmed

To garnish:
4 lemon wedges
5 cm (2 inch) piece daikon (Japanese radish), peeled
and grated

Using tweezers, remove all the bones which are hidden in the centre of the mackerel fillets. Place the fillets skin side down on a board and cut slightly on the diagonal into slices about 2.5 cm (1 inch) thick. Put the shoyu in a shallow dish with the sake and ginger juice and mix well. Add the mackerel slices, cover, and leave to marinate for about 10 minutes, stirring occasionally to ensure the slices of fish are evenly coated.

Drain the mackerel thoroughly, then coat in some of the cornflour. Heat the oil in a deep-fat frier or deep frying pan to 160°C/325°F and deep-fry the mackerel slices until golden brown. Remove from the oil with a perforated spoon and drain on paper towels. Keep hot.

Coat the mushrooms in the remaining cornflour. Add to the hot oil and deep-fry for 1 minute. Remove and drain as for the mackerel slices. Arrange a few slices of mackerel and 2 mushrooms on each of 4 warmed individual plates. Garnish each serving with a lemon wedge, and some of the grated daikon. Serve immediately.

Note: Tatsuta-age is a method of frying. In this recipe the fish is marinated before frying to give it extra flavour. Any type of fish, meat or poultry, can be used. To obtain ginger juice, grate fresh root ginger, then squeeze out the juice.

Salt Grilled Fish; Salmon with Sake Lees

Miso Marinated Fish

Sakana no Misoyaki

4 fillets sea bream, haddock, whiting or mackerel
salt
parsley sprigs, to garnish

Miso marinade:
500 g (1 lb) shiromiso (white soy bean paste)
100 ml (3½ fl oz) mirin (sweet rice wine)

Place the fish fillets, skin side down, on a wire rack. Sprinkle with salt, then leave for at least 1 hour.

Put the miso and mirin in a bowl and mix with a wooden spoon. Spread half of this mixture evenly over the bottom of a medium-sized roasting tin and cover with a piece of fine cheesecloth. Lay the fish fillets directly on the material, then cover with another piece. Spread the remaining miso over the material so that the fish fillets are sandwiched between layers of miso. Cover the tin and leave the fish to marinate overnight.

The next day, remove the fillets from the pieces of cheesecloth and pat dry with paper towels. Preheat the grill and the grill rack. Meanwhile, cut decorative slits in the skin of the fish, either on the diagonal or in the form of a cross. Place the fish on the preheated grill rack and grill under moderate heat until light brown. Turn the fish over and grill on the other side. Serve hot, garnished with parsley sprigs.

Note: Meat, especially beef, can be marinated in the same way as the fish used here, in which case use red rather than white miso, and add 2 tablespoons sugar to produce a stronger marinade. The miso can be used a second time if you add a small amount of fresh miso, and even after the second time it can still be used to make miso soup.

52

Sardine Balls

Tsukune

500 g (1 lb) sardines, defrosted if frozen
2 spring onions, finely chopped
1 egg
1½ tablespoons sake (rice wine)
½ teaspoon ginger juice (see note, Marinated Mackerel page 50)
pinch of salt
2 tablespoons vegetable oil
1½ tablespoons shoyu (Japanese soy sauce)
1½ tablespoons mirin (sweet rice wine)
10 Japanese bamboo skewers

Scale and gut the sardines and chop off the heads. Using your fingers, remove the bones from the belly. Place the sardines on a board, skin side down. With a sharp pointed knife, separate the flesh from the skin. Finely chop the flesh, or work in a food processor for a few seconds, then place in a bowl.

Add the spring onions, egg, sake, ginger juice and salt to the sardines, then mix well together. Using your hands, form the mixture into 20 small balls.

Heat the oil in a heavy-based frying pan, add the sardine balls and fry over high heat until golden brown on all sides. Lower the heat, mix together the shoyu and mirin and pour over the balls. Remove from the heat and cool slightly, then arrange 2 balls on each bamboo skewer. Serve at room temperature.

Note: If you find the texture of the mixture too soft to form into balls (which is quite likely if you are using frozen sardines), add 1–2 teaspoons cornflour to thicken the mixture and make it more manageable.

Cod Cooked in Earthenware

Tara-chiri

750 g (1½ lb) cod fillet
225 g (8 oz) firm tofu (bean curd)
225 g (8 oz) spinach
7.5–10 cm (3–4 inch) square konbu (dried kelp)
2 thin leeks, washed and sliced

To serve:
4 spring onions, finely chopped
momiji-oroshi (Plain Fried Plaice, page 48)
4 lemon wedges
shoyu (Japanese soy sauce)
plain boiled Japanese rice

Cut the cod into chunky 5 cm (2 inch) squares, retaining the skin. Cut the tofu into bite-sized cubes. Wash and trim the spinach, then cut into 5 cm (2 inch) lengths.

Put the konbu in a donabe (earthenware pot) or flameproof casserole and fill two-thirds full with cold water. Bring to the boil and immediately remove the konbu. Transfer the donabe or casserole to a portable cooking stove on the dining table. Bring to the boil and add the cod, tofu, spinach and leeks.

Each diner makes a 'dip sauce' in his or her own bowl by mixing together spring onions, momiji-oroshi, a squeeze of lemon juice and shoyu to taste. Pieces of food are then taken from the pot and dipped into the bowl of sauce before eating. Rice is served separately.

Note: At the end of the meal, season the liquid remaining in the pot with salt, shoyu and lemon juice to taste, then add some boiled rice or noodles. Serve as a soup.

Assorted Raw Fish served with boiled rice

Assorted Raw Fish

Sashimi

750 g (1½ lb) mixed fresh fish (see note)
1 teaspoon wasabi (green horseradish) powder
shoyu (Japanese soy sauce)
5 cm (2 inch) piece daikon (Japanese radish), peeled
and shredded
plain boiled Japanese rice, to serve

Gut the fish, then wash it well. (In the case of squid, clean it and remove the ink sac, as if ready for cooking.) You can ask the fishmonger to skin and fillet the fish for you, or do this yourself. Do not wash the fish again after it has been filleted, or it will be too wet and not have a good texture for serving raw; simply pat the fillets dry with paper towels before slicing and serving.

Slice the fish with a very sharp knife. Fish such as sole or plaice should be paper thin; sea bass and bream 1 cm (½ inch) thick. Tuna needs to be cut into bite-sized pieces 5 mm–1 cm (¼–½ inch) thick. Skin squid, octopus and cuttlefish, then cut into strips 5 cm (2 inches) long and 5 mm (¼ inch) wide.

Put the wasabi powder in an egg cup, add 1 teaspoon cold water and stir; the consistency should be firm, but not lumpy. Keep the egg cup well covered until serving time, or the pungency of the wasabi will be lost.

Pour the shoyu into individual shallow dishes.

To serve: arrange the different fish decoratively on a large serving platter or board and garnish with the shredded daikon. Mould the wasabi into a small mound and place on the serving platter or board. Guests should mix a little of the wasabi with shoyu, then dip a slice of fish into this 'sauce' before eating. Boiled rice is eaten between mouthfuls of sashimi to cool down the palate – the combination of wasabi and shoyu is quite hot and salty.

Note: Sashimi is a general term for prepared raw fish, *sashi* meaning 'to stab' or 'cut', and *mi* meaning 'body' or 'meat'. It can be served as a starter but this recipe is served with rice for a main course. You can use tuna, salmon, lemon sole, Dover sole, sea bass, sea bream, mackerel, prawns, squid, cuttlefish, bonito, carp, trout or even salmon roe. Whichever fish you choose, it must be very fresh, and you need to serve at least 3 different types to make an interesting main-course Sashimi. Look for the freshest kinds available on the day: the fish should have clear, bright eyes and scales; avoid any squid or cuttlefish that is reddish in colour.

Deep-fried Fish and Vegetables

Tempura

8 headless uncooked prawns, defrosted if frozen
1 medium squid, cleaned
1 large red pepper
8 button mushrooms, halved
1 large carrot, peeled
100 g (4 oz) French beans, trimmed
1 small aubergine, trimmed and sliced
100 g (4 oz) mangetout, trimmed
vegetable oil for deep-frying
plain flour for coating

Batter:
1 egg
75 g (3 oz) plain flour
25 g (1 oz) cornflour

Tentsuyu sauce:
200 ml (7 fl oz) Soup Stock (page 12)
50 ml (2 fl oz) shoyu (Japanese soy sauce)
50 ml (2 fl oz) mirin (sweet rice wine)

To serve:
2.5 cm (1 inch) piece fresh root ginger, peeled and grated
5 cm (2 inch) piece daikon (Japanese radish), peeled and grated
1 lime, cut into wedges

Wash and shell the prawns, retaining the tail shell. Remove the black vein from the back of the prawns, then make a slit along the belly to prevent the prawns curling during cooking. Skin the squid and cut in half. With a sharp knife, make fine diagonal slits on the outside to prevent curling during cooking. Cut the body into 5 × 4 cm (2 × 1½ inch) pieces. Cut the pepper lengthways into quarters; remove the seeds, then halve each piece of pepper to make 8 bite-sized pieces. Halve the mushrooms. Cut the carrot into 5 cm (2 inch) pieces, then cut each piece lengthways into slices. Make a cut at both ends of each slice almost to the opposite end, then twist the strips in opposite directions to make a decorative triangle.

Make the batter immediately before frying: mix the egg and 100 ml (3½ fl oz) ice-cold water in a bowl, then sift in the plain flour and cornflour. Mix very briefly, using 2 pairs of hashi (chopsticks) or a fork. Do not over-mix: there should still be lumps in the flour.

Put a wire rack over a roasting tin and place by the side of the cooker. Heat the oil in a deep-fat frier or deep frying pan to about 160°C/325°F. Dip the pieces of pepper in the batter so that only the inside is coated, then deep-fry skin side up for about 30 seconds, then drain. Repeat with the carrot, mushrooms, clusters of French beans, slices of aubergine and the mangetout.

Increase the temperature of the oil to about 180°C/350°F. Hold the prawns by their tails and dip them into the batter one at a time (do not batter the tail shell).

Deep-fry for about 1 minute, then remove and drain. Coat the squid pieces with flour, dip them in the batter and deep-fry in the hot oil for 1 minute. Remove and drain.

To make the sauce: bring the stock to the boil in a small saucepan with the shoyu and mirin, then pour into 4 small bowls. Arrange the fish and vegetables on a bamboo dish or serving platter with the grated ginger and daikon. Garnish with lime wedges and serve immediately, with the bowls of sauce. Each person mixes ginger and daikon to taste with some of the sauce, then dips the tempura into the sauce before eating.

Note: Tempura is a famous Japanese fish dish, sometimes described as the Japanese answer to fish and chips! Take care not to over-mix the ingredients for the batter – the idea is to make a very light, lumpy batter, not a sticky, runny one. If you can manage to mix the batter with 2 pairs of hashi (chopsticks), you will find this gives you exactly the right consistency. Do not deep-fry the ingredients for longer than stated in the recipe as they will continue to cook after they have been removed from the oil.

Fish Stew

Chiri Nabe

15 cm (6 inch) piece of konbu (dried kelp)
1.75 litres (3 pints) water
225 g (8 oz) filleted red snapper, cod or other white fish, cut into serving pieces
1 bunch of spring onions, sliced diagonally
4 fresh shiitake mushrooms, stems removed, or button mushrooms
1 block tofu (bean curd), cut into 2.5 cm (1 inch) chunks
4 large napa (Chinese cabbage) leaves, cut into 5 cm (2 inch) pieces

Dipping sauce:
120 ml (4 fl oz) shoyu (Japanese soy sauce)
175 ml (6 fl oz) lemon juice
seasoning suggestions: minced spring onions, toasted sesame seeds, freshly grated root ginger, grated white daikon (Japanese radish), shichimi

Rinse the konbu, wipe with a damp cloth and place in a fondue pan or electric frying pan. Add the water, bring to the boil, then add the fish. Bring back to the boil and add the spring onions, mushrooms, tofu and napa. Bring back to the boil, stirring constantly. The vegetables should then be crisp and tender and the fish cooked through.

To make the dipping sauce: mix together the shoyu and lemon juice, then add suggested seasonings according to taste. Divide between individual dishes.

Serve the fish stew hot, with the dipping sauce and steamed rice.

Note: This dish can be prepared at the table like a fondue, if wished. Guests should eat from the pan, lifting out the cooked morsels with chopsticks and dipping them into the sauce.

Deep-fried Fish and Vegetables

Seafood and Vegetable Salad

Umi–no–sachi Salad

3 fresh shiitake mushrooms
1 small lettuce, leaves cut into 2.5 cm (1 inch)
squares
3 radishes, thinly sliced
1 cucumber, cut into thin strips 2.5 cm (1 inch) long
1 × 15 cm (6 inch) piece of udo (spikenard), cut into
2.5 cm (1 inch) squares (optional)
2 × 200 g (7 oz) cans tuna fish, crabmeat or shrimps,
drained and flaked

Dressing:
250 ml (8 fl oz) prepared vinaigrette dressing
100 g (4 oz) sesame seeds, crushed
few drops of shoyu (Japanese soy sauce)
few drops of Soup Stock (page 12)
few drops of mirin (sweet rice wine)

Drop the mushrooms into boiling water and boil for 2 to 3 minutes. Drain and cool, then slice thinly. Place all the vegetables in cold water and leave for about 15 minutes or until crisp.

Meanwhile mix together the ingredients for the dressing in a screwtop jar and shake well.

Drain the vegetables and arrange in a serving dish. Pile the fish on top and pour over the dressing. *Serves 6*

Prawn and Rice Salad

Ebi to Gohan no Salad

625 g (1 lb 6 oz) steamed rice
1 × 425 g (15 oz) can bean sprouts, drained
2 sticks celery, sliced diagonally
½ green pepper, cored, seeded and diced
1 × 150 g (5 oz) can water chestnuts, drained and
sliced
500 g (1 lb) prawns, cooked, peeled and chopped
4 tablespoons seasoned rice vinegar
4 tablespoons vegetable oil
4 tablespoons shoyu (Japanese soy sauce)
2 spring onions, thinly sliced

Place the rice, bean sprouts, celery, green pepper, water chestnuts and prawns in a bowl and fold together gently. Cover and chill for at least 30 minutes.

Mix together the vinegar, oil and shoyu and pour this dressing over the salad. Add the spring onions and toss well. *Serves 6*

Seafood and Vegetable Salad

Steamed Fish with Ginger

Mishi Zakana

1.5 kg (3 lb) white fish fillets, cut into serving pieces
1 tablespoon grated fresh root ginger
2 teaspoons salt
4 spring onions
5 tablespoons vegetable oil, warmed
5 tablespoons shoyu (Japanese soy sauce)
spring onion shreds, to garnish

Rinse the fish and pat dry with kitchen paper towels. Arrange the fish on a heatproof plate and sprinkle over the ginger and salt. Place the spring onions on top. Cover and steam over boiling water for 10 minutes or until the fish flakes easily when tested with a fork.

Remove the fish from the steamer and discard the whole spring onions. Drain any liquid from the plate. Mix together the oil and shoyu and pour over the fish. Garnish with the spring onion shreds and serve with steamed rice. *Serves 6*

Fish Rice

Sakana Gohan

2 dried shiitake mushrooms
1 × 350 g (12 oz) white fish, cleaned
1 litre (1¾ pints) water
4 tablespoons sake (rice wine)
salt
675 g (1½ lb) medium-grain rice
4 spinach leaves or parsley sprigs
350 ml (12 fl oz) Soup Stock (page 12)
¼ teaspoon shoyu (Japanese soy sauce)
1 leek, cooked and finely chopped, to garnish

Soak the mushrooms in water for 25 minutes.

Cut the fish into three portions crossways. Place in a saucepan, head, bones and all, and pour over the water. Bring to the boil and simmer until the fish will flake easily when tested with a fork. Lift out the fish with a slotted spoon and flake the flesh, discarding all skin and bones. Set the fish aside.

Strain the cooking liquid and return to the pan. Stir in the sake and 1¼ tablespoons salt and bring to the boil. Add the rice, stir, and bring back to the boil. Add the flaked fish, cover tightly and cook for about 20 minutes or until the rice is tender and has absorbed all the liquid.

Meanwhile drain the mushrooms and trim off the stems. Drop the mushroom caps and spinach or parsley into boiling water and simmer until tender. Drain.

Pour the stock into the saucepan in which the vegetables were cooked and stir in the shoyu and ¼ teaspoon salt. Bring to the boil. Stir in the mushrooms and spinach or parsley and keep warm.

Divide the fish rice between individual bowls and pour over the stock mixture. Sprinkle the leek on top.

Lobster and Vegetables in 'Fried Armour'

Kabuto-age

2–3 dried shiitake mushrooms
1 × 1 kg (2 lb) cooked lobster
1 small carrot, cut into shreds 2.5 cm (1 inch) long
1–2 canned bamboo shoots, cut into 2.5 cm (1 inch) strips
1 teaspoon shoyu (Japanese soy sauce)
1 teaspoon sake (rice wine)
½ teaspoon sugar
1 tablespoon Soup Stock (page 12)
1 egg
pinch of salt
vegetable oil for frying
few cooked peas
4 tablespoons dry breadcrumbs
lemon slices, to garnish

Soak the mushrooms in water for 25 minutes. Drain, discard the hard stems and shred the caps.

Remove the meat from the body and claws of the lobster, discarding the intestinal vein and all soft matter in the body and at the top of the head. Reserve the body shell. Shred the meat.

Cook the mushroom caps and carrot in boiling water for 2 minutes and drain. Return the vegetables to the saucepan and add the bamboo shoots. Mix together the shoyu, sake, sugar and stock. Pour over the vegetables and mix well to coat.

Lightly beat the egg with the salt. Lightly oil a small frying pan, pour in the egg and stir until just scrambled. Remove from the heat and mix in the vegetables, peas and lobster meat. Pack into the lobster body shell and press the beadcrumbs over the top. Heat oil in a deep frier to about 195°C/385°F and fry the stuffed lobster shell until golden brown and piping hot. Drain and serve garnished with lemon slices. *Serves 1*

Grilled Clams

Yaki Hamaguri

120 ml (4 fl oz) shoyu (Japanese soy sauce)
120 ml (4 fl oz) sake (rice wine)
4 tablespoons condensed black bean soup
3 tablespoons sugar
24 clams, steamed and removed from shells
2 tablespoons vegetable oil

Mix together the shoyu, sake, soup and sugar in a saucepan. Bring to the boil, stirring. Remove from the heat.

Dip the clams in the shoyu mixture, then arrange them in one layer on an oiled baking sheet. Grill for about 2 minutes on each side. Serve with the remaining shoyu mixture as a dip.

Cod Teriyaki

Tara no Teriyaki

4 cod steaks

Tare sauce:
2 tablespoons shoyu (Japanese soy sauce)
2 tablespoons mirin (sweet rice wine)
1 tablespoon sake (rice wine)
1 tablespoon sugar

First make the sauce: put the shoyu, mirin, sake and sugar in a small saucepan and boil for 1 minute. Remove from the heat.

Thread each cod steak on to 2 lightly greased metal skewers, then cook the fish under a preheated hot grill until lightly browned on both sides. Remove from the grill and brush with some of the tare sauce. Return to the heat and cook until the tare dries. Repeat with more sauce until it is all used up. Turn the skewers in the fish each time you remove them from the grill, to prevent them sticking to the fish.

Remove the skewers from the fish, then place the fish on 4 warmed individual plates. Serve immediately.
Note: Do not skin or bone the cod steaks, or they may fall apart during cooking. Serve with 500 g (1 lb) Brussels sprouts which have been cooked in lightly salted water for 3 minutes, then stir-fried in a little butter and sprinkled with salt – they should still be firm.

58

Fish and Soy Bean Curd

Nioroshi

350 g (12 oz) white fish fillets
cornflour for coating
750 g/1½ lb silken tofu (bean curd), each cake cut into 4 pieces
vegetable oil for deep-frying

Sauce:
600 ml (1 pint) Soup Stock (page 12)
5 tablespoons shoyu (Japanese soy sauce)
3 tablespoons mirin (sweet rice wine)
finely grated daikon (Japanese radish), squeezed dry

To garnish:
finely chopped spring onion
lemon slices

Coat the fish lightly with cornflour. Wrap the tofu pieces in a cloth and pat lightly to remove excess moisture. Heat the oil in a deep-frier to 180°C/350°F. Fry the fish and tofu pieces until golden brown and cooked through.

Meanwhile make the sauce. Place the stock, shoyu and mirin in a saucepan and bring to the boil. Remove from the heat and stir in the grated daikon.

Drain the fish and tofu pieces on kitchen paper towels and arrange on a plate. Pour over the sauce and garnish with spring onion and lemon slices.

Egg-battered Sardines

Iwashi no Nishiki-age

8 medium-sized fresh sardines
salt
2 parsley sprigs, finely chopped
2 eggs
1 teaspoon mirin (sweet rice wine)
plain flour for coating
2 tablespoons vegetable oil
4 lemon wedges, to garnish

Cut the heads off the sardines, then gut the fish and wash thoroughly in lightly salted water. Open up the sardines and take out the bones with your fingers. Sprinkle salt very lightly over the fish.

Put the parsley in a shallow dish with the eggs, mirin and ¼ teaspoon salt. Beat well to mix. Coat the fish lightly with flour, then dip into the beaten egg mixture.

Heat the oil in a heavy-based frying pan, then add the fish and a little of the egg mixture remaining in the dish. Fry over low heat until lightly browned, then turn the fish over, cover the pan with a lid and continue cooking over the lowest possible heat for 2 to 3 minutes. Arrange the sardines on a warmed serving platter, garnish with lemon wedges and serve hot.
Note: The Japanese word *nishiki* means 'colourful' or 'glittering' – the egg batter gives a glittering effect.

Spring Onions with Scallops and Miso

Nuta Negi

2 bunches of spring onions, root ends removed
3 strips of wakame (dried young seaweed) (optional)
15 fresh scallops, poached and chopped into large pieces

Sauce:
3 tablespoons shiromiso (white soy bean paste)
3 tablespoons Soup Stock (page 12)
1 tablespoon rice vinegar
1 tablespoon water
1 teaspoon dry mustard

Drop the spring onions into a pan of boiling water. Boil for 2½ minutes, then drain and squeeze out the excess moisture. Cut into 5 cm (2 inch) lengths.

Soak the wakame in water to cover for 10 minutes. Drain, rinse under cold running water, then drain and cut into thin strips.

To make the sauce: put all the ingredients in a pan and stir well. Cook for 3 minutes until quite thick, stirring constantly.

Put the spring onions, wakame and prepared scallops in a bowl, pour over the sauce, then fold gently to mix. Transfer to individual serving dishes and serve at room temperature.

Prawns with Spinach and Water Chestnuts; Fish and Soy Bean Curd

Prawns with Spinach and Water Chestnuts

Ebi no Yasai-itame

350 g (12 oz) uncooked large prawns
2 tablespoons vegetable oil
3–4 sticks celery, sliced diagonally
2 onions, thinly sliced into rings
225 g (8 oz) spinach leaves, washed and trimmed
4 tablespoons shoyu (Japanese soy sauce)
300 ml (½ pint) Soup Stock (page 12) or chicken stock
2 tablespoons cornflour
freshly ground black pepper
1 × 225 g (8 oz) can water chestnuts, drained and sliced

Peel the prawns, remove the black vein, and halve them lengthways. Heat the oil in a large frying pan or wok. Add the prawns and stir-fry for 1 minute or until pink. Add the celery and onions and stir-fry for 2 minutes. Lay the spinach on top, cover and cook for 1 minute.

Mix together the shoyu, stock, cornflour and pepper to taste. Add to the pan with the water chestnuts and

bring to the boil, stirring. Simmer for 2 minutes or until clear and thickened. Serve hot, with rice. *Serves 6*

Prawn-stuffed Mushrooms

Urauchi Shiitake

30 dried shiitake mushrooms
250 ml (8 fl oz) Soup Stock (page 12)
1½ tablespoons shoyu (Japanese soy sauce)
1 tablespoon sugar
350 g (12 oz) cooked peeled prawns, minced
1 egg white
1 teaspoon cornflour
1 teaspoon salt
cornflour for coating

Soak the mushrooms in water for 25 minutes. Place the stock, shoyu and sugar in a saucepan and bring to the boil. Remove the stems from the drained mushrooms, then add the caps to the simmering liquid. Cook until well flavoured, then drain.

Mix together the prawns, egg white, cornflour and salt to make a paste. Coat the insides of the mushroom caps lightly with the cornflour, then stuff with the prawn paste. Steam for 10 minutes until hot. *Serves 4 to 6*

Snacks & Desserts

In Japan, desserts are not served with everyday meals. Sweet snacks and fresh fruit are more often served between meals rather than as part of a meal. Such sweets as dry confectionery and cakes are made from native ingredients – rice, rice flour, red beans and seaweed 'gelatine'. The Japanese also make good use of abundant fresh fruit, which is always served in prime condition and beautifully presented.

Red Bean Soup with Rice Dumplings

Zenzai or Shiruko

225 g (8 oz) azuki beans
275 g (10 oz) sugar
½ teaspoon salt

Dango (dumplings):
½ package mochiko (glutinous sweet rice flour)

Pick over and wash the azuki, then put them in a pan with 1.5 litres (2½ pints) water. Bring to the boil, then lower the heat and simmer for 2 hours until the beans are soft.

Add more water to the pan to make the liquid up to 1.2 litres (2 pints) (some of the water will have evaporated during cooking). Add the sugar and salt and cook for 15 minutes, stirring occasionally.

Meanwhile, make the dumplings: mix the mochiko with enough water to make a stiff dough. Knead well, then pinch off tiny portions to form small balls, about the size of marbles. Make a small indentation in the side of each dumpling.

Bring the azuki soup back to the boil, then drop the dumplings into the soup. Cook until the dumplings rise to the surface. Divide between warmed individual bowls. Serve hot.

Note: This soup is served as a sweet snack.

Red Bean Cakes

Yokan

2 × 425 g (15 oz) cans red kidney beans, drained
500 g (1 lb) sugar
2 tablespoons salt
1 block of kanten (agar-agar)
450 ml (¾ pint) water
1 egg white
2 tablespoons redcurrant jelly

Purée the beans in a blender or food processor, or press through a sieve. Mix the bean purée with half the sugar and the salt, stirring until the sugar has dissolved.

Put the kanten in a saucepan, cover with the water and leave to soak for 20 to 30 minutes. Bring to the boil, stirring until completely melted. Add the remaining sugar and return to the pan. Add the bean paste, egg white and jelly and stir well, until thoroughly mixed. Boil the mixture down to a gluey, starchy residue. While still liquid, pour into a square metal pan. Leave to cool and set, then cut into rectangles. Chill before serving.

Peach 'Gelatine'

Momo no Kanten

1 long kanten (agar-agar)
450 ml (¾ pint) water
350 g (12 oz) sugar
120 ml (4 fl oz) fresh peach pulp
juice of ½ lemon
2 egg whites

Wash the kanten under cold running water, then put in a pan, cover with the water and leave to soak for 20 to 30 minutes. Bring to the boil over moderate heat until completely melted, then add the sugar and stir until dissolved. Strain through a very fine sieve, then stir in the peach pulp and lemon juice and leave to cool.

Beat the egg whites until stiff, then gradually fold in the cooled peach liquid. Pour into a shallow tin and chill in the refrigerator until set. Cut into 2.5 cm (1 inch) squares or diamond shapes. Serve chilled. *Makes 24*
Note: Serve with tea, either as a snack or a dessert. Unsweetened crushed pineapple may be substituted for the peach pulp, if liked.

Green Tea Ice Cream

Matcha Ice Cream

600 ml (1 pint) vanilla ice cream, softened
1 tablespoon matcha (powdered green tea)
1 can sweetened azuki beans (optional)

Blend together the ice cream and matcha, then freeze until required. Scoop into individual serving dishes and top with sweetened azuki beans, if liked.
Note: This ice cream, with its pale, minty colour, makes a beautiful ending to a Japanese meal.

Green Tea Ice Cream; Peach 'Gelatine'

61

Apple 'Gelatine'; Almond Creams with Apricot Sauce

Almond Creams with Apricot Sauce

Almond Cream no Anzu Sauce-soe

1 tablespoon gelatine, dissolved according to
packet instructions
100 g (4 oz) sugar
pinch of salt
2 eggs, separated
300 ml (½ pint) milk
½ teaspoon almond essence
250 ml (8 fl oz) double cream
toasted flaked almonds, to decorate

Sauce:
350 ml (12 fl oz) apricot juice
100 g (4 oz) sugar
1 teaspoon lemon juice
75 g (3 oz) dried apricots, chopped

Place the gelatine, half the sugar, the salt, egg yolks and milk in a saucepan and heat gently, stirring, until the gelatine has completely dissolved and the mixture is smooth. Remove from the heat and stir in the almond essence. Chill until the mixture is beginning to thicken.

Beat the egg whites until frothy, then gradually beat in the remaining sugar and continue beating until stiff and glossy. Whip the cream until thick. Fold the cream and egg whites into the egg yolk mixture. Divide between eight moulds each with a 150 ml (¼ pint) capacity. Chill until set.

To make the sauce, place all the ingredients in a saucepan, cover and simmer for 20 to 25 minutes or until the apricots are tender. Chill.

To serve, pour the sauce over the almond creams and top with flaked almonds. *Serves 8*

Tofu Ice Cream

Tofu no Ice Cream

500 g (1 lb) tofu (bean curd)
3 tablespoons honey
¼ teaspoon vanilla essence
pinch of salt

Place 350 g (12 oz) of the tofu, the honey, vanilla and salt in a blender or food processor and process for 1 minute or until smooth. Pour into a covered container and freeze overnight.

Purée the remaining tofu until smooth. Break the frozen mixture into small chunks. Add, a few at a time, to the puréed tofu, processing at high speed. When all the frozen mixture has been added and the mixture is thick and smooth, the ice cream is ready to be served.

Red Bean Buns

Manju

500 g (1 lb) sugar
250 ml (8 fl oz) water
350 g (12 oz) flour
1 teaspoon matcha (powdered green tea)
2 × 425 g (15 oz) cans red kidney beans, drained
2 tablespoons salt

Put half the sugar in a bowl with the water and stir to dissolve. Sift the flour and tea into the bowl and mix to make a smooth dough.

Purée the drained beans in a blender or food processor, or press through a sieve. Mix the bean purée with the remaining sugar and the salt. Strain this bean paste.

Divide the dough into small portions and flatten each into a small round sheet. Shape the bean paste into small balls and place one ball in the centre of each dough sheet. Wrap the dough around the paste ball to enclose it completely. Steam the buns inside a wet cloth over boiling water for 15 minutes.

Apple 'Gelatine'

Ringo no Kanten

2 blocks of kanten (agar-agar)
450 ml (¾ pint) water
450 ml (¾ pint) apple juice
pinch of salt
½ lemon, thinly sliced
pinch of dried peppermint leaves
prepared fruit in season, such as strawberries, melon, pears (optional)

Put the kanten into a saucepan, cover with the water and apple juice and add the salt, lemon slices and peppermint. Bring to the boil, stirring, and simmer until the kanten has completely dissolved.

Strain into a bowl. Allow to cool slightly, then add the fruit, if using. Pour into a decorative mould and chill until set. *Serves 6*

63

Sponge Cake

Kasutera

5 eggs, beaten
150 g (5 oz) sugar
75 g (3 oz) honey
75 g (3 oz) plain flour
¾ teaspoon baking powder
2 tablespoons icing sugar, to decorate

Put the eggs in a bowl, then gradually beat in the sugar and honey. Beat for about 10 minutes until thick and pale, using an electric beater if possible. Sift the flour and baking powder together, then fold gently into the egg mixture.

Pour the mixture into a greased and floured 23 cm (9 inch) square cake tin. Bake in a preheated moderate oven (180°C/350°F, Gas Mark 4) for 30 minutes. Leave the cake in the tin for 10 minutes, then transfer to a wire rack and leave to cool completely.

Sprinkle with icing sugar. Cut into squares before serving. *Makes one 23 cm (9 inch) cake*

Note: This cake was originally introduced several centuries ago by the Dutch traders who came to the port of Nagasaki. In recent years, small electric ovens have become part of the Japanese kitchen, making it possible for cakes such as this one to be baked at home.

Tofu Fruit Whip

Tofu to Kudamono

350 g (12 oz) tofu (bean curd), chilled
225 g (8 oz) prepared strawberries, peaches or pineapple
1 tablespoon honey
chopped nuts, to decorate

Place the tofu, fruit and honey in a blender or food processor and process until smooth. Serve in small dishes, topped with chopped nuts.

Index